SECRETS
of
MEDITATION

ALSO BY DAVIDJI

Audio and Digital Downloads

davidji Guided Meditations: Fill What Is Empty; Empty What Is Full,
featuring Snatam Kaur and Damien Rose

davidji Guided Meditations: Opening to Love; Healing Your Heart

davidji: Come Fly with Me:
The Passenger's Guide to Stress-Free Travel

davidji Guided Meditations: Journey to Infinity: A Vibrational Myth,
featuring Dean Richards & MJ Vermette

Winter Feast for the Soul: 40 Days of Meditation & Metta

The Five Secrets of the Sweetspot: Rituals for Daily Meditation

Classroom Meditations: Student Tools for Attention, Concentration,
Test-taking, and Confidence

davidji Guided Affirmations: Fill What Is Empty; Empty What Is Full

The Chopra Center's 21-Day Meditation Challenge™

davidji Guided Affirmations: Channeling the Universe Through Your
Chakras, inspired by the Tulku Jewels Chakra Amulet Collection

davidji Guided Affirmations: Conscious Choices in Life and Love

SECRETS of MEDITATION

A Practical Guide to Inner Peace and Personal Transformation

davidji

HAY HOUSE, INC.
Carlsbad, California • New York City
London • Sydney • Johannesburg
Vancouver • Hong Kong • New Delhi

Published and distributed in the United States by: Hay House, Inc.: www.hayhouse
.com® • *Published and distributed in Australia by:* Hay House Australia Pty. Ltd.:
www.hayhouse.com.au • *Published and distributed in the United Kingdom by:* Hay
House UK, Ltd.: www.hayhouse.co.uk • *Published and distributed in the Republic
of South Africa by:* Hay House SA (Pty), Ltd.: www.hayhouse.co.za • *Distributed
in Canada by:* Raincoast: www.raincoast.com • *Published in India by:* Hay House
Publishers India: www.hayhouse.co.in

Cover design: Shelley Noble • *Interior design:* Nick C. Welch
Interior illustrations: Courtesy of the author

The author donates all proceeds from this book to charity.

The author gratefully acknowledges and credits the following for the right to
reprint material in this book:
"Sandayu the Separate," by Patti Smith, from *Babel*; used in gratitude with permission from Patti Smith.
"There Is a Wonderful Game," from *I Heard God Laughing: Renderings of Hafiz*;
used with sweet permission from Daniel Ladinsky. Thank you for being so gracious
about my interpretation of your interpretation of Hafiz's interpretation of God.
Bhagwan Shree Rajneesh on the Fool, written by Osho from *Dang Dang Doko
Dang*; used in gratitude with permission from the Osho International Foundation.

Library of Congress Cataloging-in-Publication Data

davidji.
  Secrets of meditation : a practical guide to inner peace and personal transformation
/ davidji. -- 1st ed.
     p. cm.
  ISBN 978-1-4019-4030-0 (tradepaper : alk. paper) 1. Meditation. I. Title.
  BL627.D385 2012
  158.1'2--dc23

                                    2012011857

Tradepaper ISBN: 978-1-4019-4030-0
Digital ISBN: 978-1-4019-4031-7

16 15 14 13   9 8 7 6
1st edition, September 2012
6th edition, September 2013

Printed in the United States of America

"It all has to come from inside, though, I guess."

— JIMI HENDRIX

DEDICATION

This book is dedicated to my dear friend, loving brother, and relentless teacher, David Simon, an amazing being who has touched my life and my heart in more ways than one could ever imagine. He flows through me in each breath I take. He is in my heart with each day's meditation, each sunset I drink in, each herb I pick, and each tender moment I witness. Among the countless number of lifelong lessons he has shared with me, he taught me that in each moment and in each interaction we have with people, animals, and our beloved mother earth, we have a choice to leave behind either toxic residue (known in Sanskrit as *ama*) or nourishing vital nectar (known as *ojas*). This is a lesson I am still learning each day, and it has helped me evolve my emotional intelligence and awaken my emotional digestive fire so that I could move beyond much of my constricted conditioning, make more nourishing choices, and share more selflessly with the world.

I have always trusted his heart, and that has taught me to trust mine.

When the sky is dark and the stars are out, it brings me back to the innocence and sweet atmospheric vibration of our morning hikes and late night strolls. I think about how deeply we shared in hundreds of quiet conversations as we toured the world from Dublin to Vancouver, Miami to Alaska, London to Whistler, Oxford to Los Angeles, and everywhere in between—with the universe as our witness, we shared our hearts, our dreams, our truest essence. The stars tell the whole story every night . . . and they will forever.

David introduced me to Daniel Ladinsky's interpretations of the great Sufi poet Hafiz. The poem "There Is a Wonderful Game" speaks so sweetly of our undying connection. Please accept it in deepest reverence.

There is a game we should play,
And it goes like this:

We hold hands and look into each other's eyes
And scan each other's face.

Then I say,
"Now tell me the difference you see between us."

And you might respond,
"Hafiz, your nose is ten times bigger than mine!"

Then I would say,
"Yes, my dear, almost ten times!"

But let's keep playing.
Let's go deeper,
Go deeper.
For if we do,
Our spirits will embrace
And interweave.

Our union will be so glorious
That even God
Will not be able to tell us apart.

There is a wonderful game
We should play with everyone
And it goes like this . . .

To you, my timeless Sufi master, may you laugh and love with Hafiz every day.

CONTENTS

FOREWORD

No doubt you've heard the expression "Silence is golden." Yet in this modern era, treasuring the experience of a quiet mind has not been that resonant in our world consciousness. As a practitioner of meditation for many decades and as a physician dedicated to healing and transformation, I've learned the value of meditation as a tool for quieting the mind is inestimable.

The message that most of us received from an early age is that an active mind is a valuable mind. We clearly need the skills of an awake and creative mind to function, create, achieve, accomplish, and enjoy life. At the same time, the value of a quiet mind is tremendous, though less commonly recognized or appreciated. When the thoughts and noisy chatter of the mind settle, we have access to deeper levels of awareness. And when we can combine these two skill sets—the active mind that allows us to explore the world of form and phenomena and the quiet mind that brings clarity and balance into our awareness—we are in the best position to determine how to direct our energies and make the most evolutionary choices that will serve us, humanity, and the planet.

In this beautiful book, davidji—a sweet yogi and a dedicated teacher—explores various technologies to help bring the mind from chaos to quietude. Along the way, you will awaken to deeper levels of stillness in your bodymind and effortlessly develop a regular practice. Taking time on a daily basis to go within and access the field of pure awareness brings us from activity to silence, from individuality to universality, and from the personal to the universal. Meditation is like a bath for the mind; it allows our mind to be clear and refreshed and to see the same experience from a slightly different point of view. This shift expands our capacity for happiness, well-being, love, and creativity.

The information lovingly contained within these chapters will help you find your pathway to expansion. I encourage you to explore and try the practices that most resonate with you. Then you will fulfill the purpose of meditation, which is to transform your sense of self from constricted to expanded. As you awaken your body, heart, mind, and soul, you and all those in your life will benefit.

— **David Simon, M.D.**
Co-founder of the Chopra Center for Wellbeing

PREFACE

It is my hope that you meditate. It is my belief that we will change the world through meditation. It is my understanding that connecting to the stillness and silence within allows each of us to live life with expanded awareness, deeper compassion, and greater fulfillment. It is my experience that time spent in stillness and silence can open your heart to the true depth of your universal essence. Accessing this depth of pure, unbounded consciousness on a regular basis has allowed me to *see* and *feel* the world with an ever-expanding openness, deeper empathy, greater clarity, and a heightened connection to source. At this point in my life, I think this is a good thing.

Aham brahmasmi is a Sanskrit expression meaning "I am the universe." When we can genuinely feel we are not in or of this world but rather the whole world is within us, we slowly begin to integrate that mind-set into our words, our thoughts, and our deeds. Once this is truly how you feel (and daily meditation will awaken that understanding), you will effortlessly tap into the limitless supply of what the universe has to offer you—a wellspring of effortless abundance; an unfolding of deeper fulfillment; and a sweeter, more loving world that you can walk through with greater grace and ease.

No different from when you are in a dream state, every experience you have in your waking state is self-derived, self-created, self-influenced, and self-motivated. This is not to say things outside of you don't happen; rather, it's how you respond to the unexpected or the uncertain—what you do with new information and old rituals—that becomes the fabric of your life. And we all respond to everything: a kiss on our lips, the wind on our cheek, a diagnosis, a text, a cough, a comment, a sigh, a desire, a memory, a caress, the ringing of a phone, the honking of a horn, the wink of an eye, a fleeting thought, footsteps in the distance, the sun on our neck, the tone of an e-mail, the color of someone's hair, and even the reading of this sentence. Yet there is no such thing as an external force that can *make* us feel a certain emotion or respond in a certain way.

Our moods, feelings, and emotions are multidimensional interpretations based on our conditioning. Most of it is probably imprinted into our subconsciousness before we reached our teens. The remainder is embedded over the past few decades as we drank life in and reinforced those early interpretations, weaving them into the fabric of our being. Our response to each moment is a blend of that conditioning, our DNA, our current circumstances, our emotional intelligence, and our state of mind in that instant.

Meditating every day has taught me that we are all the masters of each moment. And effortlessly weaving this practice into every fiber of my being has given me tools and techniques for living life with less stress and anxiety, greater clarity and focus, expanded compassion and empathy, deeper love and more frequent joy, and a viewpoint that is more receptive to other perspectives, which offers me increased possibilities. I believe that anyone who is willing to embrace meditation can access these tools as well. Feel free to consider this book your meditation tool kit.

I thank you for taking the time to read this book, which came from my heart. I encourage you to try meditating and begin a meditation practice using the guidance contained in these pages. I hope you'll let me help you find what you are looking for. I would consider it a privilege.

Peace.

davidji

PART I

AWAKENING TO NEW POSSIBILITIES

Although I practice a particular type of meditation, I honor all schools of meditation. The gentle drifting from outside ourselves to inside and then back out again is one of the most magnificent processes a human can experience. As your thoughts, your breath, and your physiology slow and progressively quiet to more subtle expressions, your awareness will expand—at first during meditation and then in your life outside of meditation—which will awaken a world of infinite possibilities in every moment.

I am not a monk or an evangelist of any particular religion. I live in the real world, and my meditation training occurred under real-world circumstances. I wrote this book to share my journey to wholeness, which I found through meditation. Wholeness is available to anyone who desires to tap into the stillness and silence that rests within. I offer myself and these teachings to beginners and masters alike. I am humbled by the thought that more than a million seekers throughout the world have joined me in this voyage of profound reconnection. I invite you to join the celebration with those who have found greater purpose, clarity, compassion, fulfillment, healing, flexibility, love, dharma, creativity, peace, abundance, one-ness, transformation, and joy through the daily practice of sitting in stillness and silence . . . and those who are taking their first step right now.

How to Use This Book

This book is designed as a meditation owner's manual. I suggest you read it once through from beginning to end, participating in all the exercises and guided meditations. When you have finished, you will have a deeper understanding of meditation, you will have experienced many different types of meditations, you will have gone beyond any description that one could share, and you will have felt the rich benefits of a daily practice as your life unfolds with joy and a calming ease that perhaps has eluded you. If you find yourself drawn to a particular form of meditation, I encourage you to explore it further: do online research, find a class, read more, and see where it goes. If you are interested in having a personal guide in Primordial Sound Meditation, reach out to me or any of the 1,500 Chopra Center–certified instructors around the world, and find one with whom you resonate. More information about finding a teacher can be found in the meditation resources section on my website, **davidji.com**. Challenge what you are told about experiences, and explore them for yourself. Keep trusting your heart.

As you stumble on information that makes sense to you, feel free to make notes, highlight, and dog-ear the pages providing guidance or information with which you connect. And, of course, feel free to share the love with anyone who is ready to begin a practice.

A Word about Language

Many of these teachings were first articulated in Sanskrit, the ancient language of India, and Pali, the ancient language of Buddhism. I have shared the original languages as well as the translations and transliterations into English. I encourage you not to torture yourself over pronunciation or grammar. There is an entire vocabulary of meditation, and the goal is for you to meditate rather than become a walking meditation encyclopedia. Eventually, these words will become woven into the fabric of your daily language, and in the meantime, these pages can be a helpful resource for learning to speak *consciousness as a second language.*

CHAPTER ONE

SEARCHING FOR THE GURU

---

*"What keeps life fascinating is
the constant creativity of the soul."*

— DEEPAK CHOPRA

How do you spell guru?
JEEE . . . You . . . Are . . . You!
I began to meditate 31 years ago, while attending college in upstate New York. I was young, impressionable, and a curious reader, who had stumbled onto five books that changed my life: (1) the *Bardo Thodol* (known in English as *The Tibetan Book of the Dead* or *The Tibetan Book of Living and Dying*); (2) the ancient Vedic text called the *Bhagavad Gita;* (3) *The Teachings of Don Juan,* by the mystical storyteller Carlos Castaneda; (4) the consciousness classic *Be Here Now,* by Ram Dass; and (5) *The Way of Zen,* by the brilliant British philosopher Alan Watts. This group of books, some dating back more than 3,500 years and some as current as this century, opened my eyes to new answers to some of my fundamental life questions: Who am I? Why am I here? Is this real? What is reality? Why are we all here? What does it all mean? Is there more?

Reading these books also led me to my first meditation experience—an extra-credit weekly Zen meditation session offered to the students enrolled in an experimental Eastern philosophy course I was taking. The 12 of us sat in a circle, and our Zen master walked clockwise around us. We had been instructed that when we noticed a thought drifting into our mind, we were to raise our hand. In his hand, the Zen master carried an 18-inch bamboo stick known as a *keisaku.* On seeing one of our hands rise, our teacher would gently nod, silently walk over, and thwack the hand-raiser on the back with his keisaku. I don't know if it stopped the thought, but it certainly created a new one.

I found deep stillness and several cosmic moments in those sessions, but I also had lots of thoughts. Ouch! I only lasted in that school of meditation two weeks. I found myself *not* raising my hand to avoid the thwack of the keisaku . . . and when you find yourself lying to your Zen master, that's when it's time to move on. As Alan Watts once said, "When you get the message, hang up the phone." I had gotten the message. But I wasn't really sure what to do with it. *What now?* I asked myself.

Over the next 30 years, I would explore many other forms of meditation, occasionally resonating with a particular modality enough to comfortably practice it for extended periods of time. But with the same ease that I would drift into a practice, I would drift away from it as work, home, relationships, the corporate world, and life's twists and turns spun me in varying directions, ultimately bringing me to my knees.

The Journey from Biofeedback to Mindfulness

After moving on from Zen, I embraced biofeedback for a few years. Biofeedback is a practice in which you focus on slowing your breath and controlling your heart rate. I got really good at it, and for the first time ever, experienced a deep sense of relaxation in my life. But my pulse became so low that I kept passing out in elevators whenever I went above ten stories.

I then moved on to a series of techniques that took me from listening to sound waves to Kundalini dancing to gazing at candles to energy healing to contemplative prayer to following my breath to the exotic tantra and ultimately to meditating with a mantra. The word *mantra* comes from two Sanskrit words: *man,* which means "mind," and *tra,* which means "vehicle or instrument." So our mantra is our mind vehicle . . . our mind instrument. It is a tool to transport the mind from a state of activity to one of quieting down into stillness and silence.

Then there was the period when I embraced mindfulness meditation—the meditation of the Buddha. I figured if it was good enough for the Buddha, it certainly was good enough for me! In mindfulness meditation, we keep bringing our awareness to all the experiences of the present moment—thoughts, sounds, physical sensations, our breath . . . whatever comes . . . wherever our attention goes in the moment. We keep coming back to the present moment—not the past, not the future, but the present—where we ultimately become the silent witness, witnessing ourselves in every moment. This is similar to the practice of breath awareness meditation and is one of the most practiced types of meditation on the planet as millions of Buddhists practice it each day. Even the word *mindful* has become somewhat trendy in the West over the last decade as it has been a euphemism for meditation that sidesteps the cultish misconceptions and stigmas of traditional meditation.

Virtually every yoga class ends with some form of mindfulness meditation, lying on our back in *savasana* (or corpse pose), bringing closure to the class, totally surrendering to the moment, relaxing our body, and letting our mind simply drift into gratitude as all the benefits of the practice are integrated into every fiber of our being.

For many years, mindfulness practice was my primary form of meditation. But just as it was becoming trendy, I stopped meditating.

Sleepwalking Through Life

I worked for many years in the world of finance and business amid the wild corporate swirl of New York City. I had even worked for a time on one of the higher floors of Tower Two, at what is now referred to as Ground Zero. But one day I realized—as my life was spinning out of physical and emotional balance—I had stopped meditating. I had replaced my 5 A.M. meditation ritual with an early morning train ride into the bowels of the World Trade Center, and I had replaced my evening meditation with a double scotch. And like that . . . *poof* . . . my practice had disappeared.

Also gone were the balance and deep fulfillment I had felt during my meditation days. I was living to work, to fill an empty part of me that I had forgotten. It had been a decade since I had slept through the night. Instead, I often awoke at 2 A.M. with a painful knot in my stomach that stayed there through the day and into the evening. I brought it to bed with me every night. I ate my lunch at my desk while texting on my "crackberry," chatting on my cell phone, typing e-mails, and wolfing down a sandwich . . . all in five minutes. And I realized I had been doing that for almost 15 years.

Nonstop overwhelming thoughts relentlessly raced through my head as I attempted to juggle so many different pieces of my life and finding unfulfillment at every turn. I craved peace of my mind. I craved a job with a purpose. I craved the depth of feeling I had known so well in my youth. I was light-years from that moment. I was sleepwalking through my life. My personal and work relationships were stressed and strained. I was waking up, burning through the day, performing my "job," coming home, eating dinner, reading a book or watching TV, and passing out. My personal and home lives had been taken over by my career. And my career had been taken over by a zombielike autopilot of an existence. I felt empty, adrift from any guiding principle, deeply in pain, purposeless, and unenlightened about what my life had become and where it was headed. I started to question my accomplishments and the value I contributed to those in my life.

And so one day in SoHo, as I walked past a row of cardboard boxes in which homeless people were living, a grizzled hand reached out and grabbed my pant leg, and a curious, soot-covered face peered up at me and asked, "What's gonna be on your tombstone?" I stopped in my tracks (as my aimless gaze narrowed to a pinpoint, zeroing in on the man's crystalline blue eyes) and reflected on my life as his tender hand slowly slid down my ankle and dropped to my shoe. Face to face, soul to soul—connected in a transcendent, cosmic moment, it took my breath away. I was staring into the face of God. Oh my God! Tears came to my eyes. We locked gazes for what seemed like eternity, and I mouthed the words to him, "I don't know." My mind was a tsunami of thoughts, memories, and desires. My gaze then passed through him . . . through everything until there was nothing. I wandered aimlessly for hours after that, his pointed words reverberating through every cell in my body. What *was* going to be on my tombstone? What *was* my purpose? I felt like a prisoner living eternally on death row, stuck in a painful purgatory with no reason for being.

My mind was overflowing with smoke-filled images of the collapse of Tower Two, just blocks south of the downtown office building where my staff and I had stood on the roof and watched in horror on that fateful day. So many we knew and loved and so many more we'd never get to know. For me, the psychological fallout from 9/11 drifted somewhere between emptiness, a profound sense of emotional grief, and a primal wake-up call—the deep need to live a purpose-driven life. But I was light-years from knowing what that purpose was or having it actualized in my current trajectory.

That night, as I shared my day's story with my wife over dinner, she handed me a piece of paper. She had sensed my daily pain and had explored a few deeper options for me to consider. One was Seduction of Spirit, a meditation retreat in England with Deepak Chopra. She encouraged me to follow my heart. A work colleague advised me, "Jump and the net will appear." One of my yoga teachers suggested, "Quit your job today. The universe will provide."

I followed my heart and jumped. One week later, I learned my meditation mantra; one month later, my job evaporated into the ether; and two months later, I headed off to Oxford to meet Deepak Chopra and learn about the concept of *dharma*—my purpose in life. It was there I learned that the word *guru* is a Sanskrit term for "remover of darkness," essentially one who teaches enlightenment. But no one else can actually make you "see." They can help you open and awaken to what already rests within, essentially giving you permission to access aspects of yourself you had previously not given yourself permission to awaken. Maybe you didn't know they were there. Maybe you did but were unsure how to access them. But once you do awaken to the stillness and silence that rest beneath the layers of activity in your daily life, you will know it's there and forever available to you. Like a choppy, turbulent, stormy sea that surrenders to the calming, tranquility of a still, serene pond, in meditation, the active mind progressively slows to more subtle levels of quietude. Each day, when your meditation is over, you will be able to "listen" to life with greater appreciation and understanding and to live your life with greater grace and ease.

Awakening to Stillness

In early 2002, I left New York City—which I had often referred to as "the center of the universe"—to spend a week with spiritual advisor Deepak Chopra, meditating in the land of Harry Potter. The previous month, an Indian meditation teacher living in London had crossed the pond for the weekend and taught me and six other students a modern translation of an ancient practice known as Primordial Sound Meditation. During an intensive three days, I learned about the foundations of this timeless tool and was walked through an understanding of my physical body, my subtle (psychological) body, and my causal (or spiritual) body. I then received my Primordial Sound mantra based on the moment of my birth and was taught how to practically apply a meditation practice in my daily life that would ready me for the upcoming retreat.

When I arrived in Oxford for the Seduction of Spirit meditation retreat, I immersed myself deeply into stillness and silence along with 75 seekers from around the world, looking to tap into clarity, truth, awareness, and love. Most of the attendees were from England, Ireland, Scotland, and Wales, but a good 30 of them hailed from other European cities, like Geneva, Rotterdam, Copenhagen, Munich, Barcelona, Istanbul, Paris, Milan, Helsinki, Prague, Brussels, and Stockholm . . . all speaking the universal language of consciousness!

Deep, deep into meditation we went from sunrise to sunset and then after dinner. In just a few days, my heart opened wider than it ever had before, and I let go of every preconception I ever had about meditation. I surrendered to the process Deepak personally laid out for me. I felt its full power. It was as if my heart were made of soft white linen that had been immersed in black India ink . . . so thick and heavy . . . so black . . . so dark and so painful. And each day of the retreat, it was as if I were draping that white linen heart through a running stream, washing it, cleansing it, purifying it of that blackness . . . lightening the load . . . a little less pain and a little more clarity. As I peeled away the conditioned layers of my life, new thoughts emerged, expanded aspects of my self awakened, and I connected for the very first time to my soul. I cried. I laughed. I tapped into the collective. I came face to face with my unconditioned self and experienced the infinite one-ness of the universe. I fell in love again—with myself, with everyone, with life.

By day four, the blackness was gone. We were meditating for more than five hours a day, and every moment felt surreal. I felt reborn. I reconnected with my heart, which had been closed for so many years. I awakened to a long-hidden forgiveness and made long-overdue amends with some of the deepest wounds of my past—things I'd done and not done that I regretted, ways of thinking and living that had not served others, relationships that had gone undernourished or become painful, paths I'd walked that had turned into dark rabbit holes, and sweet people with tender hearts along the way whom I had hurt. And I began to explore my most important relationship—the one I have with my true Self—the stillness and silence that rests within my soul . . . the core of my being . . . my essence . . . pure unbounded consciousness. I found surrender. I embraced detachment. I touched a part of my being long dormant, and I realized how easy it was for me to access the power of my source through meditation.

But I still had so many questions, and I continued to believe that the answers were out there, so on the last day of the retreat, I headed off to India to continue my search for the guru. The vivid first impressions of my midnight landing in Delhi resonate with me still. The cabin doors opened, revealing a moonless, hazy sky. As I walked down the steps onto the runway, I took my first deep breath of India. It felt sweet . . . musty . . . humid . . . fragrant . . . new . . . fresh . . . ancient . . . familiar . . . and exhilarating.

As a taxi took me to my hotel, the outskirts of India unfolded as we approached the city. And very quickly, I was in the thick of it, absorbed into the one billion strong fabric of the magic that is India. I continued the daily routines I had learned at the Oxford retreat. I meditated and prayed every day. I practiced yoga each morning. I performed rituals of gratitude and charity. I bathed in the Ganges River in Varanasi as smoldering, cremated bodies drifted past me. I traveled east to Bhodgaya and sat under the bodhi tree, where Buddha first attained enlightenment. I met with the *naadi* leaf reader in Swamimalai, who read me the details of my past, present, and future lives scrawled in the enduring language of Old Tamil on an ancient preserved palm leaf, even revealing to me the exact moment of my death in this lifetime.

In the town of Jaipur, I experienced *shaktiput,* a form of energetic awakening that blew my mind for weeks and continues to weave through me with regularity so many years later. I visited the spiritual guru Sathya Sai Baba in his Abode of Supreme Peace—the Prasanthi Nilayam ashram—where he sprinkled me with holy ash called *vibuthi,* which he had manifested out of thin air.

I then headed off to the Koregaon Park ashram in Pune, founded by the magnificently irreverent and provocative swami Osho, then known as Bhagwan Shree Rajneesh. Osho had left this earthly plane several years before, but it was in Pune that I stumbled on his quote, "Truth is within you; do not search for it elsewhere." But that didn't really make sense to me at the time, so I continued to search elsewhere.

I traveled north to Dharamsala in the Himalayas to hear the Dalai Lama speak about loving-kindness, but he was in deep meditation. (It would be seven more years before I would have the privilege to meet His Holiness and be able to truly appreciate his divine eloquence, deep compassion, and love-filled energy.)

Light at the End of the Tunnel

In search of the guru, I trekked thousands of miles south, all the way down India's belly to the Meenakshi Sundareswarar Temple in the 2,500-year-old city of Madurai. Within the vast walls of this huge ancient structure the size of a small village and honeycombed with statues, shrines, prayer halls, thousands of Technicolor painted deities, a room with one thousand pillars, and a sacred pond, I was squeezed among a rapturous, barefoot throng of more than 20,000 devotees of the Hindu god Lord Shiva and his wife, the goddess of compassion, Parvati.

As the waves of devotion washed through the crowd, I suddenly found myself totally alone before the holy pond. It was if the swarm of pilgrims had abandoned the city for the moment. Slowly, a figure stepped from the shadows and walked into a beam of sunlight. His silhouette had a corona around it, radiating so brilliantly that I had to shield my eyes. He introduced himself as Mr. Jinghan, a Brahmin priest who had traveled 1,500 miles south of his Punjab village in the north on a pilgrimage to meet *me*. That's right . . . *me!* "Mr. David, we've been waiting for you a very long time. Shall we sit together?"

I looked behind me to see how many of the 20,000 pilgrims had found their way into the sacred shrine. Miraculously, we were alone. In this vast stone-encased hallway where billions had visited, prayed, and meditated over the last thousand years, there were only the two of us . . . and the sound of our beating hearts. And without ever meeting each other, he claimed he had traveled all this way to see me! I closed my eyes and bathed in the warm radiance Jinghan projected into the room.

We sat for a few minutes as he chanted a prayer to the Divine Mother to awaken the feminine creative power in our hearts. Within moments, his mumblings drifted into the ether, and I slipped into the gap. The last thing I remember was feeling my heart crack open and going deeper than I ever had before as everything merged into one. When I opened my eyes, I was alone. Tears were streaming down my cheeks, a profound sense of well-being rippled through me, and Jinghan was gone.

I glanced down at my watch. Hours had passed, and the sun had drifted much lower on the horizon as the late afternoon melted into evening. Thousands of candles and butter lamps that had been invisible in the daylight suddenly bathed the room, tickling the walls in a light show of dancing shadows and flickering images. I gazed into the vast still pond before me, reflecting the night sky's billions of stars seamlessly melting into the tens of thousands of tiny hand-lit flames that surrounded its tranquil edges. I noticed my own flickering reflection in the belly of a silver Shiva statue that sat two feet in front of me. My amorphous rippling image reflected back at me—shrinking, stretching, distorting, expanding, and vanishing in the darkness as if I had no body; I was a vibrating mass of light. I was transfixed on my image and then I had none.

The minutes merged into hours; thousands of pilgrims trekked past me in the darkness, and sensation slowly flowed back into my body. Something caught my eye on the tile beneath my knee as I uncrossed my legs. Looking down, I spied a magnificent gold locket in the shape of the elephant-headed god Ganesh. The gold-faced, so-called Remover of Obstacles was suspended from a black cotton cord. Jinghan must have placed it next to my knee while I was drifting through the cosmos. I lifted it to eye level and bowed my head in reverence. Then I bent my head into it as if being anointed and slid on the necklace. Like a halo, it surrounded me and then fell gently around my neck, heralding this moment of profound connection to source.

As my awareness returned to the present moment and physical sensations returned to my body, I realized everything in the hall was framed by a radiant halo. Then I became aware of all the people in the room. Hundreds of pilgrims had poured into the room, and each of them had a radiating aura as they squeezed past me on all sides on their way to the sacred pond. I squeezed the locket in my hand, pressed it tightly to my heart, and began giggling as I recounted Jinghan's words: "Mr. David, we've been waiting for you." I slowly rose to my feet, and within seconds, I was merged into the teeming mass of devotees, physically and spiritually, as I saw them all as a reflection of my own soul . . . all divine . . . all God. It was in that moment I first felt the tangible energy and infinite power of *the collective,* which has transformed the way I now see the world.

Vibrating from the intense rippling of the devotional intentions that emanated through the temple, I joined a wave of thousands of pilgrims traveling even farther south to the sacred beaches of Kanyakumari, at the southernmost tip of India. There we prayed to the mother goddess under a constellation-filled sky and a new moon; I was blanketed in darkness as I lay in a shallow tide pool, rippling with the subtlest movements of the warm, starlit sea before us.

I continued on my journey, spending my days in search of a guru to validate my transformation, chatting with roadside *rishis,* traveling from temple to temple, praying in the inner sanctums, bathing in holy lagoons, practicing yoga on moonlit beaches, receiving *diksha* enlightenment blessings, and meditating with each sun's rising and setting. Yet finding no greater truth than the timeless waves before me, I traveled east along the shore until I reached the coastal island of Rameshwaram, where I tried to spy the mythological monkey god Hanuman re-creating the ancient tale of the *Ramayana* by leaping across to the island of Sri Lanka on a bridge of monkeys. But I never saw him.

We Are the One We Are Seeking

For six months, I searched high and low for my guru. And one morning, as I lay in a hammock in a tropical cashew forest in Kerala, surrounded by the most intense symphony of wild bird calls and reading from a worn copy of the Bhagavad Gita, I read Chapter 2, Verse 48, for what seemed like the very first and the four millionth time all at once. I found myself mouthing the words that Lord Krishna shares with the mighty warrior Arjuna: "'*Yogastha kuru karmani*' . . . Established in one-ness, perform action." And as I read, a profound and powerful message silently swept into me, beneath my thoughts and into every cell at once, cutting through the energetic curtain of forest life. All sound stopped; the cashew trees froze; the parrots morphed into stillness; my body had no borders, no skin to encapsulate what I felt; the rushing sense of well-being surged into my physical body and expanded to my mind. Then came something way deeper and more profound than any thought or experience. In a flash, everything became one, and I instantly understood. How do I put it in just a few words? **The guru is inside.**

Yes, the guru is inside. Deep . . . deep . . . deep inside, housed by this flesh casing we call a body and trapped for a lifetime within the constrictions of our five senses and our mind that interprets each moment. Peel away those layers, go deep inside, and deeper still . . . and at our very core, our essence is pure, vast, unbounded consciousness. Infinite. It had been a long buildup over many years and multiple lifetimes of experience that brought me to my aha! moment. But I had touched something, connected to something, actually *been* something beyond me—beyond us—something so expansive I could not fathom its edges. Yet, at the same time, I was it, and it had no limits. It was as if I had amnesia and suddenly remembered everything all at once. I describe it as finding another gear in perception; one that you always had but of which you were unaware. This shift came to me at once and resonates still at this very moment.

Accessing the Divine Within

What I realized that day was that we are indeed human expressions of the divine universe. We absorb existence through our senses, distill it with our intellect, and what flows out is a persona— an ego—a sense of self that individuates us from one another. When we look to our most genuine selves, beneath the layers of the ego, the intellect, the realm of our emotions, and our physical body, we can access the divine flow. In fact, the answer to every question we could ever ask ourselves rests inside. We simply need to give ourselves permission to hear the answer. And how do we access the vast unboundedness of the universe beyond our conditioned existence? How do we surrender to become the calm amid the chaos? How do we reach beyond this lifetime of conditioning to experience the sweet, silent stillness that rests within? The most effective and powerful tool for expansion and transformation that I have found is the timeless practice of daily meditation.

Each of us has an innate ability to slow our mind and body, disconnect from activity, and visit the depths of our unconditioned self. We are gifted with the aptitude to experience our very soul and go beyond time and space—to transcend this earthly plane of existence and then bring a little piece of tranquil one-ness back into this realm, allowing us to be happier, more compassionate, more forgiving, more creative, more intuitive, and more connected to who we are and the divinity that rests within each of us.

I almost fell out of my hammock as I leaped up in response to my aha! moment. I packed my bag, checked out of my room, walked to the bus station, traveled the 1,400 miles to Mumbai, and 25 hours later I was boarding a plane back to New York City. Intermittently throughout the 22-hour flight, I drifted in and out of meditation. One thing was clear: My life would never be the same. There was no going back. I had actually experienced universality and could not close my eyes to the infinite one-ness of the universe. And the practical lesson was even more profound. By drifting from a state of activity to a state of stillness and silence, I so easily and effortlessly accessed the realm of one-ness. And I had finally learned that by doing nothing—*no thing*—present-moment awareness will gently flow into my daily life . . . into my waking state . . . even into my dream state.

I had finally "gotten" it. Halfway through my life, I had come to discover a part of myself that had been dormant since my early childhood. Deep, deep within, I was reintroduced to my still point—my unconditioned Self. I experienced the universal that was within me. *I had finally found the guru!*

Tapping into Silence

Since that moment, not a day has passed when I do not dip my toes into the ocean of stillness that rests within me. Since learning Primordial Sound Meditation, I have meditated every morning and almost every night, and my life has unfolded with purpose, clarity, deeper fulfillment, lightness, and an overall sense of well-being that flows through me in each moment. This daily reconnection has provided me with profound emotional expansion that has led me to make more conscious choices in my interactions with the world, with my friends and loved ones, and with myself.

Meditation has gracefully infused me with the inherent knowledge that in each moment, I have the ability to choose to be reflective rather than reflexive. I am not bound by my lifetime of conditioning. I have infinite possibilities in every thought, word, and action. And I always have a choice. In fact, in every decision, I have a choice between a grievance and a miracle. This expanded internal point of reference has created within me a more open and accepting orientation to everything around me. My spiritual transformation is ever flowing. I don't know where it goes from here or where it will end when I leave this earthly realm, but for now, I choose meditation and its profound daily gifts.

Sharing the Gifts of Meditation

On returning from India, I immersed myself even more deeply into the timeless teachings of meditation—so much so that almost everyone who knew me suggested I become a meditation teacher. Acquiescing to the constant recommendations of my friends—specifically Rookie Komitor, who had also been at the meditation retreat in Oxford—I enrolled in the Chopra Center's Primordial Sound Meditation teacher training and the requisite mind-body workshop, where I would be immersed in Ayurveda (the 5,000-year-old science of life) under the guidance of Deepak Chopra and his partner of 20 years, neurologist David Simon. During that mind-body workshop, David Simon and I had an instant love connection, and it was on July 14, the last day of Journey into Healing, that I pledged my life and heart to expanding the work done by David and Deepak and raising the vibration of their translations and teachings. The very next day, I unplugged from my life on the East Coast, moved to Carlsbad—a sunny beach town in Southern California, 30 miles north of the Mexican border—and volunteered for six months to serve the needs and desires of the goddess known as the Chopra Center for Wellbeing.

In the decade since that moment exploded through every cell in my body, I have immersed myself in the timeless teachings of meditation, Ayurveda, yoga, Vedanta, emotional healing, and the ancient wisdom of consciousness. Throughout those ten years, I have dedicated myself to whatever role Deepak and David felt I could add the most value. With the loving support and grace of the Chopra Center's founders, I was named chief operating officer, then director of marketing and sales, and then lead educator at all the events. Ultimately, after years of study and practice, I was chosen as the first dean of Chopra Center University. In that role, I was given the opportunity to merge the co-founders' modern translations with my real-world interpretations, rituals, and techniques and help students who also live in the real world to learn, share, teach, and master this timeless body of knowledge. In addition to the hundreds of thousands I have taught in person at workshops and retreats, through my CDs and downloads, and through my online meditations and programs, I have helped empower more than 1,000 teachers in more than 50 countries to share this ancient wisdom with their families, co-workers, students, and communities throughout the world. That alone is one of the most fulfilling experiences of my adult life.

Those who have embraced these wisdom teachings and timeless practices make up the global fabric of meditators—not only swamis, yogis, rinpoches, lamas, saddhus, nuns, and monks but also doctors, lawyers, soldiers, businessmen and businesswomen, brokers, dancers, nurses, firefighters, administrators, professors, CEOs, artists, mothers, fathers, singers, drivers, writers, caregivers, kids, bikers, police officers, directors, salespeople, scientists, musicians, nannies, homemakers, taxi drivers, investment bankers, homeless people, prisoners, contractors, veterans, entrepreneurs, secretaries, trainers, pilots, waiters, retirees, screenwriters, bass players, directors, technologists, psychiatrists, assistants, house-keepers, accountants, chefs, developers, vice presidents, performers, life coaches, office workers, healers, managers, politicians, athletes, actors, truckers, stylists, therapists, teachers, and those in hospice. They have all learned how to integrate these timeless teachings into their day-to-day lives. They have transformed the world by transforming themselves.

I have personally witnessed the transformation of thousands of my students as they have moved from panic and anxiety to confidence and calm, from fear and anger to self-love and self-worth, from confusion to clarity, and from emptiness to deeper fulfillment. I have sat at the feet of the masters of meditation and Vedic wisdom and received some of the most powerful translations of these timeless teachings. I have made my daily practice the cornerstones of my day. And I have witnessed an uplifting sea change within my own being and a transformational thread in each day. Students tell me they feel a natural unfolding of deeper compassion for those in their lives, a greater clarity about life in general, a more universal perspective that weaves through each thought, and a continuous shift in their perspective on existence and this life of ours. My hope and intention is to share that same transformation with you throughout the pages of this book. And it all begins with a meditation practice.

CHAPTER TWO

WHAT IS MEDITATION, AND WHY SHOULD I CARE?

*"Don't ask what the world needs. Ask what makes
you come alive and go do that. Because what the
world needs is people who have come alive."*

— HOWARD THURMAN

For thousands of years, people have used various techniques to bring their minds to a quieter state of being. Depending on where in the world they have lived and what their culture or society has encouraged, human beings have come up with an extraordinarily rich array of practices for going beyond the ordinary waking state to expanded states of consciousness. Depending on the culture and religious orientation, these ritualized practices include chanting, breathing, ecstatic dancing, healing touch, listening to music, making love, visual stimulation, aromatherapy, and even ruminating on the taste of chocolate. Each technique is specifically designed to move the mind from its current state of activity to one of present-moment witnessing awareness.

You have already experienced the phenomena of present-moment witnessing awareness many times throughout your life, but perhaps you didn't even realize it. These are the moments when you are in the "still zone." It's that moment on a roller coaster when you are screaming at the top of your lungs as your body plunges downward to certain death—or when you are playing sports and every shot you take, every move you make, is the perfect one. It's when you are giving that big presentation and rather than read some memorized script, you spontaneously seem to channel just the right words in an effortless flow. It's when you spontaneously say or do the perfect thing at the exact perfect moment, cook the most brilliant meal as if you were a culinary genius, make passionate love . . . merging into your partner and surrendering to the bliss of an orgasm. It's the experience of gardening in your backyard and feeling so immersed in the aroma of the soil; the vivid colors in each petal; the beauty of the moment; and the textures of the earth, plants, and flowers that time seems to stand still. And it's the pure joy of laughing so hysterically your belly starts to spasm. These are all states of present-moment witnessing awareness, when we are not thinking for one moment about the past or reaching one second into the future.

When we experience present-moment awareness in a state of restful alertness, we are experiencing the same stillness zone we experience during deep meditation . . . pure unbounded consciousness . . . the realm of no thought, no sound, and no sensation. When you are in that space, you have essentially disconnected from all the things in your world that are in the realm of activity. In the language of many meditators, this is referred to as accessing the space between your thoughts—the gap—a space pregnant with pure potential and infinite possibilities.

When you have a consistent daily meditation practice, instead of only having sporadic tastes of the bliss of present-moment awareness, you begin to experience that bliss more and more in your everyday life. As you meditate regularly, a physiological shift occurs that grows deeper, stronger, and more profound with repetition. Like building any muscle in your body, meditation is a practice that transforms your entire physiology over time. This shift is subtle at first, and as the process of physical and emotional softening occurs, you begin to view life in new and expanded ways. Life takes on a different hue . . . a deeper meaning . . . a more universal understanding that pervades every cell of your being. The present-moment awareness you experience in meditation begins to flow throughout each thought, each conversation, each keystroke, and each breath.

In both ancient and modern writings on the experience of meditation, this change, shift, or transformation of awareness—this space of *being*—has been referred to by many names, including enlightenment, transcendence, awakening, satori, the aha! moment, Brahman, rapture, bliss, being in the gap, astral projection, connecting to source, *turiya,* remote viewing, witnessing awareness, *bhagavan* or *brahmi chetana,* cosmic consciousness, God or Christ consciousness, being in the moment, *atma darshan* (glimpsing the soul), one-ness, unity, *ananda,* and *samadhi.*

And when you experience no activity within you or outside of yourself, you actually open yourself to realms of expanded consciousness and a greater depth of feeling that include higher levels of creativity, intuition, personal growth, compassion, subtle empowerment, forgiveness, and peace of mind. Whether this stillness lasts for a tenth of a second, ten seconds, or ten minutes is of no consequence. Touching stillness—even in the smallest of doses—allows you to connect to your unconditioned Self . . . to your source.

WHO ELSE MEDITATES?

All it takes is one meditation and you join the ranks of millions around the world who consider meditation to be a centering practice in their lives and something that connects them more deeply to their inner light. In addition to Deepak Chopra, David Simon, and numerous other human empowerment leaders—such as Jean Houston, Oprah Winfrey, Wayne Dyer, Louise Hay, Eckhart Tolle, Neale Donald Walsch, Marianne Williamson, and Anthony Robbins—the following people have acknowledged the importance of meditation in their lives. Some have been my teachers, others my students, and others are simply famous meditators. We are all part of the same flow, the fabric of the collective consciousness.

Jennifer Aniston, Sean Astin, Aung San Suu Kyi, Orlando Bloom, Kate Bosworth, Russell Brand, the Buddha, Gerard Butler, Jack Canfield, Kyle Cease, Beth Nielson Chapman,

Pema Chödrön, Leonard Cohen, Confucious, Sheryl Crow, His Holiness the Dalai Lama, Al Gore, Tipper Gore, Ram Dass, Laura Dern, Donovan, Ralph Waldo Emerson, Mia Farrow, Patrick Flanagan, Benjamin Franklin, Mahatma Gandhi, Richard Gere, Billy Gibbons, Sri Yukteswar Giri, Heather Graham, Ariana Grande, Tara Guber, Herbie Hancock, Thich Nhat Hanh, George Harrison, Goldie Hawn, Phil Jackson, Kathy Jarvis, Andy Kaufman, Anthony Kiedis, Jack Kornfield, J. Krishnamurti, Lao-Tzu, John Lennon, Annie Lennox, David Lynch, Madonna, Ricky Martin, Miten, Alanis Morissette, Caroline Myss, Joel Osteen, Dr. Mehmet Oz, Gwyneth Paltrow, Patanjali, Ezra Pound, Deva Premal, Jon Kabat-Zinn, Jack Kornfield, David Lynch, Moby, Rick Rubin, Meg Ryan, Susan Sarandon, Steven Seagal, Jerry Seinfeld, Swami Sivananda, Howard Stern, Dave Stewart, Sting, St. Teresa of Avila, Henry David Thoreau, The Boston Buddha, Tina Turner, Shania Twain, Alan Watts, Ken Wilber, Tal Wilkenfeld, Tiger Woods, Stevie Wonder, and Paramahansa Yogananda.

Of course, it's not necessary to be a celebrity or have a guru (other than oneself) in order to have a solid and fulfilling meditation practice. It is safe to assume that if all these high achievers meditate, chances are they share the common characteristics of people seeking balance, wholeness, healing, wellness, and the best aspects of who they are . . . their most awakened and divine selves.

The Story of You

Go back to the moment of your birth. Most likely you don't remember, but here's pretty much how it went. You emerged from the womb pure, whole, unconditioned, and perfect—with no earthly conditioning. Perhaps the doctor gently smacked you on your bottom, and from that moment on, every experience and being that touched your world—doctors, nurses, parents, siblings, best friends, boyfriends, girlfriends, exes, teachers, schoolmates, students, religious leaders, spouses, lovers, ex-spouses, friends, loved ones, bosses, co-workers, people you meet just once, even the barista who sells you your morning coffee—have layered and layered and layered you with messages and impressions. Like the ever-growing layers of an onion, you've responded with conditioning, reinforcement, and new growth . . . covering up that pure, whole, brilliant diamond in the center and influencing, molding, and blanketing you with veneers of emotional and physical conditioning.

And here you are today. It's a few years later and a few million light years from that moment of innocence, purity, wholeness, and perfection, when the light of this world first shined in your eyes. But through your meditation practice, each time you connect to your natural state of stillness and silence, you are peeling away the layers of conditioning and reconnecting to that brilliant source, dipping your toe in—dipping your fingers into that pure, unbounded, enlightened aspect of yourself.

The magnificence of meditation isn't so much the experience during the practice itself, but each time you meditate, you peel back more layers of conditioning, get closer to the radiance of the diamond inside, and bring back into your life a thimbleful . . . a teaspoonful . . . an eyedropper full of what rests at the center of your essence—pure, whole, still, silent, unconditioned, light-filled, unbounded, universal, collective consciousness, where you are not simply you; you are everyone and everything. You are one-ness.

Now maybe that sounds a bit daunting. Maybe you just wanted to learn how to sleep through the night, have less stress, find balance, breathe easier, lower your blood pressure, and live a more peaceful life. You will have that . . . and so much more simply by opening yourself to a daily meditation practice. Developing a regular meditation practice will very quickly give you observable physical and emotional benefits. But meditation is not like taking a Valium; you meditate so you don't feel the need to take antianxiety medication. Your calmness starts before the storm and keeps you feeling centered even as the winds of chaos swirl around you. And this sense of abiding peace can develop pretty quickly. Meditation can begin to improve your physical health, your emotional well-being, and your spiritual connection with your very first experience. But it will also open up a realm of self-awareness and higher consciousness that will connect you to the more universal and divine aspects of your Self.

Exploring Your Expectations

Before every class I teach, I ask each meditation student to share why they want to learn to meditate . . . what they hope to experience. Why have you chosen to embark on this path? Here's a list of the top 20 expectations and desires that my students have shared over the years:

1. Peace of mind

2. Less stress

3. To slow down the world and stop my thoughts

4. Greater clarity or intuition

5. Less anxiety

6. Lower blood pressure

7. To breathe more easily

8. Enlightenment

9. Deeper connection to Source/Self/Spirit/the Divine

10. Emotional healing and freedom

11. Awaken creativity

12. To calm the storm

13. To stop the sense of being overwhelmed

14. More restful sleep

15. Happiness

16. Deeper, more loving relationships

17. To boost my immune system

18. To ease my pain

19. To develop my ability to relax

20. To empower myself

Are there any desires on this list that resonate with you? Is there anything that you'd like more of in your life? Less of? You get to create it. Meditation can help you experience everything on this list and your deepest desires. It simply requires a daily practice. And I can comfortably assure you that within only a few days, your life and those people in it will benefit in every moment on every level from your embracing this gentle practice.

What's the reason you want to establish a daily meditation practice? What is *your* expectation? Write it down right now on the My Intentions page at the end of this book and date it. When you check back in a month or two, you'll see how you've manifested this desire in your life! I also recommend that you start keeping a journal or begin making notes throughout this book, so you can reflect on your practice when you are not reading. Try it for 30 days and see how your life unfolds.

Getting Started

Right now you have everything you need to meditate, so let's give it a go. First, find a comfortable place to sit—on a chair or couch, on the floor, a park bench—anywhere you will be relatively undisturbed by external activities.

Once you have found the place, get comfortable, relax into it, and simply become aware of your breath. Don't breathe any differently . . . just allow your awareness to drift to your breathing.

As you read these words, feel the air flow in and out of you. Feel your lungs stretch and relax. Feel your chest rise and fall. Now close your mouth, and gently breathe in and out, solely through your nose. Feel your belly fill as you inhale. Feel it release as you exhale. Again, don't consciously do anything to alter your breath other than closing your mouth and breathing both in and out through your nose. Just observe your breath for about a minute . . . simply be aware that you breathe in, hold it in for a moment or two, exhale for a moment or two, and hold that out for a moment or two before you inhale again.

As you breathe, silently notice *I'm breathing in, I'm holding the breath, I'm breathing out, I'm holding the breath.* Maintain this awareness for the next few minutes.

☙

Now become aware of your physical body . . . how does it feel? Are you hot or cold? Relaxed or tense? Do parts of your body hurt, and are there other parts you don't even feel right now? Notice that as your awareness drifts over different parts of your body, you become more aware of your physiology. Let's make our calves tingle right now. Feel the tips of your nostrils without touching them. Become aware of your lips. Isn't it funny how our awareness truly does dictate our experiences?

☙

Look at your hands right now. Look at your palms. Rest them on your thighs, and feel them come to life. Out of sight, out of mind . . . but within sight, within mind. Now bring your attention to the blood flowing into your hands. Keep your focus on your palms. Feel the blood move into your palms. Feel them begin to get warm in the center.

☙

Where attention flows, energy goes. Do you see how as soon as you become aware of something, your mind starts to interpret your experience? Do you notice how your mind instantly wants to define it, label it, categorize it, or assign it meaning? Do you see how your awareness is connected to your body as well?

Now move your awareness beyond your hands and down to your feet. Start on your right side. Flex your right foot. Wiggle it a bit. Roll your ankle around for a few moments. Now relax your foot. Feel each toe as you move your attention from each toe to the next and then from one side of your foot to the other. Feel that flow of attention move from your toes down the sole of your foot into your heel. Then move your attention slowly up the back of your calf until you arrive in your mind's eye at your knee. Now, gently breathing in and out and using only your mind, massage your kneecap in a circular motion and move around to the back of your knee. Now move up your right hamstring and energetically feel the front of your thigh without touching it. Let a relaxing sensation radiate from the top of your thigh. Slowly breathe in as you keep the attention on your thigh. Feel it. Close your eyes for a few moments and gently breathe. Feel it. Feel all the sensations and interpretations you are experiencing in your right leg.

Now bring your awareness to your left foot. Flex it. Wiggle it a bit. Roll your ankle around for a few moments. Relax your left foot, and feel each toe as you move your attention from each toe to the next and then from one side of your foot to the other. Feel that flow of attention move from your toes down the sole of your left foot into your heel. Then feel it slowly move up the back of your calf until you arrive in your mind's eye at your knee. Now, gently breathing in and out and using only your mind, massage your kneecap in a circular motion and move around to the back of your knee. Now move your awareness up your left hamstring and energetically feel the front of your thigh without touching it. Let a relaxing sensation radiate from the top of your thigh. Slowly breathe in as you keep the attention on your left thigh. Feel it. Close your eyes for a few moments and gently breathe. Feel it. Feel all the sensations and interpretations you are experiencing in your left leg.

Now let's bring our awareness to both feet. Wiggle them. Roll both ankles around a bit. Now relax your feet and let them melt into the floor. Now feel each toe on both feet as you move your attention from each toe to the next and then from one side of your foot to the other. Feel that flow of attention move down the soles of your feet into your heels. Remember to keep breathing as you drift to each part of your body. Then feel it slowly move up the back of your calves until you arrive in your mind's eye at your knees. Now, gently breathing in and out and using only your mind's eye, massage your kneecaps in a circular motion and move around to the back of your knees. Now slowly move your awareness up your hamstrings and energetically feel the front of your thighs without touching them. Let a relaxing sensation radiate from the top of your thighs. Slowly breathe in as you keep the attention on your thighs. Feel the energy in your thighs. Sit there for a few moments and gently breathe. Feel it.

Now move your attention to your pelvis. Sit with that feeling for a moment or two; simply observe it as you consciously move all of your awareness to your pelvis. Feel the blood flow in and out of your pelvic region. Feel any discomfort you have get lighter as you witness the area from the tops of your thighs to your belly button becoming more vital and warmer from the attention you place on your pelvis. Sit with this sensation for a few moments with your eyes closed.

Now drift your awareness up into your belly. Feel the blood flow into your belly. Do you see how subtly shifting your awareness has actually brought blood flow and other physiological changes to these areas? Feel the blood flow against gravity from your pelvis up into your belly.

Simply awakening the lower half of your body with your mind has brought all these body parts into your awareness. Moments ago your attention was on reading. Where attention flows, energy goes. Pretty interesting, isn't it?

Now with your breath, see if you can gently breathe and move your awareness from your belly, up your torso, to your heart. Feel the power center of your physical body—your heart—become more open and more full. Notice how right now you are able to take a deeper breath than you could before. Your ribcage can expand more with every inhale. Once you truly feel full in this region of your body, breathe in again, and as you exhale, move your attention even higher up your chest. Breathe in and pull your energy from below your heart to the area around your heart; feel the sensation in your chest. Sit with that for a few moments. Feel your heart fill with love. With gratitude. With compassion. With forgiveness. With joy. Notice as you do this . . . a smile unfolds on your face.

Now push it up even further as you inhale. At this moment, you are experiencing present-moment awareness. As your attention goes, there you are in that moment. Not thinking about the past . . . not thinking about the future. Totally present. Totally here. Right now.

Now lift your eyes from the page after you've read these directions. Look around, and take in all your eyes observe. Don't judge; just witness . . . like a video camera simply absorbing all it sees in total witness mode. Take in the colors; see the depth and shade of everything around you. The shapes . . . the distances between objects, their shadows, how the light is falling, their denseness. Just stay with this for a minute or two as you receive all these waves and particles of light that you are turning into meaning.

What do you hear in this moment? Are there noises around you? Music? Sounds of nature? Sounds of a busy world? Any internal noises, like your stomach rumbling? Or the sound of your breathing?

Remember to keep breathing through your nose as your awareness heightens. Are you aware of any aromas? What is the smell of your surroundings? Keep breathing and bring your awareness to some part of your body that feels tight or heavy or constricted. It might be your heart, belly, temples, back, legs, arms, throat, or any other area. Don't do anything other than drift your awareness to that place and ask yourself how it feels. Now with your awareness on that place, breathe in deeply to the count of three. And slowly exhale, bringing even more attention to this area. Let's do this again.

Now slowly breathe in and out three times with your eyes closed. I'll wait.

How did the experience change with your eyes closed? Did you feel a difference? Did you become aware of your thoughts? Were you thinking more or less? Did you visualize your surroundings on the back of your eyelids? Did your other senses become more aware? Did you hear better? Relax more? Did it seem comfortable or unfamiliar in any way?

And what does the area of the body you focused on feel like now? Is it a bit lighter, looser, more open? As you begin to answer this question, your mind is drifting into the past. But the present-moment awareness you experienced only moments ago is now part of you here . . . now . . . in this present moment. This whole exercise took fewer than five minutes. A daily meditation practice can deliver this to you in much greater doses on a consistent basis. Imagine how beneficial this could be.

MEDITATION CONTINUED: EYES CLOSED

Most schools of meditation instruct practitioners to close their eyes so that they will take in less activity from the visible world. We'll discuss visual meditations a bit later, but for now, let's get ready to close our eyes again. We'll be following our breath for a few moments here, so get comfortable, gently breathe, and silently notice *I'm breathing in, I'm holding the breath, I'm breathing out, I'm holding the breath. I'm breathing in . . .*

As each aspect of your breathing occurs, notice it . . . witness it . . . observe it. Feel the rising, the falling, the in, the out, the pauses between each inhale and exhale . . . and keep doing so for a few minutes. If you drift away to any other experience—such as thoughts, sounds, or physical sensations (and you will)—gently remember to return your attention to the breath and the observation that *I'm breathing in, I'm holding my breath, I'm breathing out, I'm holding the breath out.* If you'd like, you can shorten it to *In. Hold. Out. Hold.* But don't just say it robotically; actually observe each part of your breath, and narrate the experience as you live it.

Now put down your book and close your eyes. Let's meditate together using this breathing practice for three full minutes. Don't worry about timing yourself, but feel free to place a clock in front of you or look at your watch. And feel free to go longer, if you like.

Okay, I'm guessing you're back now. How did that feel? How do you feel now? Any changes? Thoughtfully answer these questions:

- Did the time seem longer or shorter than it actually was? Did it feel like 20 years? Or 20 seconds?

- Were you bored? Restless? Antsy?

- Did you feel more relaxed at any time?

- Did you feel any settling down?

- Did you fall asleep?

- Did you become aware of your thoughts? Your emotions? Your body?

- Did you find yourself judging the experience?

- Did you feel a wave of a particular emotion or physical sensation wash over you?

- Did you experience a separation or disconnect between your breathing and your repetition of "In. Hold. Out. Hold"?

- Did your awareness drift away from the breath at any time? Did you remember to gently drift your attention back to your breathing and to follow your breath?

- Did you become frustrated? Did you become lost? Did something become clearer?

- Did you see anything in your mind's eye?

- Did you notice any particular thoughts, sounds, or physical sensations that became a part of your awareness?

- Did you open your eyes to check the time or your surroundings?

- Did you see anything or feel anything that was different from what you expected? Did you notice any difference in your awareness when you were silently repeating, "I'm breathing in, I'm holding the breath, I'm breathing out, I'm holding the breath"?

All these sensations, emotions, thoughts, sounds, and experiences are part of meditation—witnessing awareness. You were actually just meditating! This type of meditation is known as breath-awareness meditation, and you just did it. What you experienced is exactly what you were supposed to experience: drifting back and forth between your breath and thoughts, sounds, and physical sensations. And when you turn this into a daily practice, your mind calms down and finds it less necessary to engage the thoughts.

Imagine if you were receiving a text or phone call every five minutes, and your ringer was on really loud. You would notice the calming effect of turning the ringer softer, even if the calls continued. And then if you turned the ringer on silent mode, even though the calls still came in every five minutes, you would be unaware, undistracted, undisturbed. Ultimately, you'd calm down and have less anxiety or stress over the incoming messages, because they wouldn't be persistently alerting you. Meditation helps you turn your personal ringer on silent mode to separate you from your thoughts and the external swirling of life. It doesn't take you out of this life; it connects you more deeply to it.

Meditation actually allows you to experience yourself more deeply without the frenetic onslaught of your mind and the external world relentlessly picking at you. Everything you thought was swirling around is still out there. But now you see it differently—more universally; you respond differently—more consciously. It is in these moments that transformation occurs. And when you can go deeper . . . and deeper still . . . so deep that there is no world, no body, no thing. For just a moment . . . a second . . . a minute . . . you transcend this time-bound body . . . you go beyond this ego-based mind. You experience pure one-ness . . . pure, unbounded consciousness . . . infinite unity. The experience isn't describable. It isn't explainable. It's beyond human comprehension and language's ability to express. We use words like *stillness, peace,* or *whole* to describe what we experience in meditation, even if just for a moment. But words fail in the invisible realm of pure, unbounded consciousness. Only the direct experience of non-duality . . . of being . . . of experiencing one-ness can genuinely convey the true definition.

Giving yourself a few breaks each day from the persistent nonstop of the realm of activity is all it takes to create major shifts in your life. I call it taking a "time in," a term first coined by Andy Kelley, "The Boston Buddha," a student of mine and a powerful meditation teacher who teaches kids in schools to connect to their own stillness and silence. The shift begins with this relatively effortless practice in which we subtly introduce stillness, which then interrupts the conditioned pattern of nonstop activity. The result is that suddenly, amid all this reinforcement of activity, there is a blip . . . a virtual millisecond of nonactivity. And it has a profound consequence.

You connect to that millisecond of stillness and silence and bring it back into this world . . . into this life . . . into each thought . . . into each moment. That's the magnificence of meditation—not what happens during the meditation but what happens in every other moment of your day. It becomes a part of who you are, and it's cumulative; it builds and builds with each sunset and sunrise, with each meditation, with each new day, with each conversation, with each person in your life, with each new thought, and with each new choice.

CHAPTER THREE

THE BENEFITS
OF MEDITATION

*"Your living is determined not so much by what life
brings to you as by the attitude you bring to life;
not so much by what happens to you as by the
way your mind looks at what happens."*

— KAHLIL GIBRAN

The physical, emotional, and spiritual value of meditation has
been well documented for thousands of years. Scientists, philoso-
phers, spiritualists, and religious leaders have heralded the power
of witnessing awareness. They may refer to it as deep reflection,
being present, contemplation, prayer, meditation, or simply relaxing, but it's all the same thing—disconnecting from the activity in
our moment-to-moment life and drifting to the space between our
thoughts. In the Yoga Sutras, written some time between 200 B.C.
and A.D. 200, the sage Patanjali (who created a common thread for all
yoga to follow) defines meditation in four Sanskrit words: *yoga chitta
vritti narodha,* which means "one-ness is the progressive quieting of
the fluctuations of the mind."

Over the first few days, weeks, and months of daily meditation,
the quieting impact that this simple practice has on your bodymind begins to be expressed in each choice you make (your shift
may be so subtle that even you don't see it at first). Your thoughts,
selections, decisions, and daily actions become more conscious,
leading to more intuitively conscious behaviors. Then one day
you realize you have a broader perspective, a deeper sense of calm,
and heightened clarity . . . yes, greater creativity, expanded grace,
greater ease. You realize you are making more spontaneous right

choices. You realize you are being more authentic; there is greater alignment between what you think, what you say, and what you do. The world is still turning—and sometimes faster than ever—but to you, that swirl is in slower motion, like texts coming into your cell phone with a really faint hum rather than a blasting ringtone.

Over time, moving from activity to stillness during meditation translates into more conscious behaviors during nonmeditation (the other 23 or so hours of your day). Your interactions with the world shift more effortlessly from reactivity to responding, from reflexiveness to reflectiveness, from defensiveness to openness, and from drama to calmer.

And there's a big bonus on top of all these other nourishing aspects of having a practice. Over time, meditation quiets you to a state where you experience life with a deeper understanding of your true Self, which can open the door to spiritual exploration, connection, discovery, and fulfillment. It is along the so-called spiritual path that you truly can experience your unbounded Self . . . your unconditioned Self . . . the infinite you that rests at the core of who you are underneath your body and beneath this worldly garb of titles, roles, masks, ego, and the complexities of this life.

In Part II of this book, we explore many types of meditation. But if you simply limited yourself to only 30 minutes a day of the breath meditation we explored in the previous chapter, you would very quickly start to observe magnificent, tangible changes in your physiology, emotional state, sense of Self, and sense of life. Your earthly body will be more aligned with your cosmic body. Maybe you feel it now from the short meditation we just practiced . . . and it will continue. And maybe you have never felt it. Regardless of the depth of your spiritual nature, you will become more imbued with the ability to open to greater possibilities in each moment instead of the one or ones you were fixed on. This creates a more universal trajectory for your life with an expanded point of view. By seeing yourself as more universal and less personal, you'll realize more options in each moment instead of seeing only the limited ones you thought you had before. Everything in your life becomes richer when you see there are lots of ways that things can play out, and your previously constricted viewpoint only made you feel more helpless as life unfolded. But this tool called meditation can give you the edge you need to feel strong each day, to gain clarity, and to finally regain your peace of mind.

The purpose of a spiritual journey isn't to change your mind; it's to *expand* your mind to understand the true potential in each moment in your life . . . to discover a Self who has the ability to see more possibilities and expanded points of view—even the ones opposing yours—and then to choose creatively . . . intuitively . . . sacredly.

Evolving Our Brains

Different types of meditation styles take you to different places. Some calm you in the moment, others calm you after the moment, some open you, some inspire you, some relax you, some expand you, others transport you, and some deliver you to a life of one-ness and deeper fulfillment. This may sound like a huge leap from the few minutes of meditation you experienced in the last chapter, but the clinical, scientific proof of the power of meditation and 5,000 years of testimonials should give you the support you need right now to continue exploring.

Over the last several years, thousands of compelling scientific studies have found evidence that a regular, consistent meditation practice can offer a wide range of healing benefits. Doing a simple Internet search of the words *meditation studies* yields more than 7,000,000 search results and more than 2,000 research papers providing evidence that meditation is a powerful tool in enhancing stress management, pain relief, restful sleep, cognitive function, and physical and emotional well-being. The data include hundreds of clinical studies performed by science and medical departments at major universities, research reports in such venerable sources as *The Journal of the American Medical Association (JAMA)* and *The New England Journal of Medicine,* and special features in more popular publications ranging from *The Wall Street Journal* to *Time* magazine to *The New York Times.*

In the January 30, 2011, issue of *Psychiatry Research: Neuroimaging,* Massachusetts General and University of Massachusetts Medical School reported results of a clinical study that demonstrated that meditation can transform our brain. Using MRI brain scans at the beginning and end of the eight-week trial, scientists discovered that each of the 16 subjects who meditated for 30 minutes every day experienced actual changes to the physical structure of their brains. Within 56 days, each subject's MRI displayed an increase in the gray matter in the hippocampus (the part of our brain responsible for learning, spacial orientation, and memory) and a reduction in the gray matter of their amygdala (the fear, stress, and anxiety center of the brain). In less than two months, the brain can change its physical structure and the way it's wired—all from a daily practice of 30 minutes.

A recent brain wave study by Dr. Richard K. Davidson at the University of Wisconsin tested meditating monks and non-meditating volunteers on their response to pain and to the threat of pain. Dr. Davidson spoke at length about this study at the Sages and Scientists conference in February of 2012. I'll distill here what he shared: he monitored the pain centers of the brain as he applied a heated applicator to the arms of the test subjects. As the heat was directly applied to the skin, all the test subjects responded similarly. When instead, the test subjects were told that pain would be applied in ten seconds, the non-meditators' pain centers reacted instantly, while the meditators' pain centers did not respond until the heat was actually applied ten seconds later. What's the takeaway here? The non-meditating world reacts first to the hint or projection of pain in the future and reacts as if it were feeling the pain. The meditators stayed in the present moment longer and did not actually *feel* pain when the threat of pain was announced.

I find this study to be the most profound insight that we can remove and lessen suffering in our lives if we don't project ourselves into the future and manufacture potential suffering. Yet most of our life is played out in the future as our hopes, dreams, wishes, and needs, weave into expectations and we start reacting to scenarios yet unborn as if we were clairvoyant.

Finally, after thousands of years of eye-rolling by nay-sayers, the value of meditation is validated scientifically in a laboratory with the most advanced technology to monitor the brain. And the results of studies like these in medical centers and institutions of higher learning continue to be published and posted online for the world to access.

Yet the most transformational results of meditation can only truly be felt by the one having the experience. That can happen with your very first meditation, and you're already there.

How Meditation Changes Our Physiology

During meditation, specific physiological shifts occur. These shifts are cumulative, and over time, they can transform the way our body and mind balance themselves and integrate with each other. The most powerful proof that meditation changes the body-mind lies at the very core of our DNA, in a primal survival response we all have shared for millennia: the fight-or-flight response.

THE FIGHT-OR-FLIGHT RESPONSE

As human beings evolved more than 20,000 years ago, we were hardwired with a self-preservation reflex known as the fight-or-flight response. It was first described by American physiologist Walter Cannon in 1929 and explains what happens to our body's most primal brain functions when we perceive a threat to our physical body—essentially how we react when something crosses our boundary of safety. When we perceive a life-threatening situation, we react in the moment and choose one of two basic paths of survival: to fight or to run.

Essentially, it works like this: Imagine that you're hunting and gathering in a jungle during prehistoric times, when you hear a saber-toothed tiger make a loud hiss. On perceiving this threat, your body's limbic system (which controls emotion, behavior, memory, and your sense of smell) immediately responds via your autonomic nervous system, a complex network of endocrine glands that automatically regulates your hormonal chemistry and metabolism. The autonomic nervous system also performs functions like the unconscious licking of your lips, the consistent blinking of your eyes, sneezing, and other functions that you usually perform automatically, without conscious awareness.

THE BODY REACTS TO A THREAT

On hearing the saber-toothed tiger, your sympathetic nervous system (which is the part of the autonomic nervous system that maintains homeostasis) rapidly prepares you to deal with what is perceived as a threat to your safety. It essentially says, "There's a good chance you will become this predator's dinner, but if you fight or run away, you could live." It then goes on a lightning quick mission to help you achieve that goal. First, you begin to perspire. Your limbic brain knows that if you do end up fighting or fleeing, you will most likely overheat, so the fastest way to bring your temperature down is by automatic sweating.

Next, your hormones initiate several metabolic processes that help you cope with sudden danger. Your adrenal glands release adrenaline (also known as epinephrine) and other hormones that speed up your breathing, spike your heart rate, and elevate your blood pressure, quickly driving more oxygen-rich blood to your brain and to the muscles needed for fighting the saber-toothed tiger or for running away.

All of this happens before you've had an intellectual conversation with yourself about the impending danger. In fact, the threat could be real or imagined, but if the limbic brain perceives it, you will automatically respond in seconds as if the threat were real.

These self-preservation processes are all triggered by the same part of your brain that regulates hunger, thirst, sexual arousal, fear, and sleep. Your energy soars as the stress hormones adrenaline and cortisol surge into your bloodstream. At the same time, your pancreas secretes a hormone called glucagon to immediately raise your blood sugar with the equivalent sugar kick of you eating several Snickers candy bars at once.

As these physiological changes take place, your senses become heightened, your heart starts racing, and all distractions, pain, thoughts, and internal conversations leave your awareness as your focus becomes concentrated on one single goal: survival.

Your bodymind starts sending very clear messages to different cell clusters and organs throughout your body: *We don't need to be thinking about growth,* and your growth hormone secretion shuts down; *we don't need to be thinking about sex,* and your sex hormone levels decrease; *we definitely don't need to be thinking about fighting germs right now,* and your immune system is suppressed. The blood flow to the largest organ in your body (your skin) is also reduced and the blood in your digestive system moves to your arms and legs so you can better fight or run. With your mind and body in this temporary state of metabolic overdrive, you are now prepared to respond to a life-threatening situation. And this will most likely be the most stressful and intense fight of your life. Your bodymind knows this and is preparing you in milliseconds.

What happens next is truly amazing. The solid parts of your blood—your platelets—begin to plump up and get stickier. Your bodymind knows you are preparing to fight whatever life-threatening entity is out there, so your blood begins preparing to clot in advance of your being cut!

As I mentioned previously, the primary area of the brain that deals with stress is the limbic system. Because of its enormous influence on emotions and memory, the limbic system is often referred to as the "emotional brain." It's also called the "old" or "early" mammalian brain, or paleomammalian brain, because it emerged with the evolution of our warm-blooded relatives and marked the beginning of social cooperation among all animals. But fast-forward 20,000 years to the present day, and there aren't too many saber-toothed tigers out there. In fact, unless you're defending your country in a war zone or in a life-threatening line of work such as firefighting or law enforcement, the daily need for the rest of us activating our fight-or-flight mode is a rarity.

This is what happens to your body during the fight/flight response:

- An increase in blood pressure, and stress on your heart
- An increase in your stress hormones (adrenaline, cortisol)
- An increase in your blood sugar (glucagon tells the pancreas to slow insulin production)
- A decrease in blood circulation especially to your digestive tract
- Decrease in your growth and sex hormones
- Suppression of your immune system
- Increase in the stickiness and plumpness of your platelets

David Simon referred to these as the seeds of illness because they lead directly to the following diagnoses: coronary heart disease, anxiety, addictions, diabetes, gastro-intestinal disorders, infections, cancer, strokes and heart attacks. Modern science is slowly discovering that chronic stress impacts the brain as well. Clinical trials on mice have demonstrated that these stress hormones affect our dendrites—the signal receivers and senders on nerve cells—by shrinking them, which impedes the easy flow of the information they are transmitting. When this occurs in our hippocampus it challenges our memory and learning ability.

Stress: How We Respond to Unmet Needs

The fight-or-flight response is referred to as a stress response. The term *stress* is short for *distress,* a word evolved from the Latin word *stringere,* meaning "to draw tight or pull apart." In English, it was first used centuries ago to describe hardship and affliction. In the 1930s, Hungarian endocrinologist Han Selye popularized the theories of stress leading to disease and 45 years later authored the classic *Stress Without Distress* in which he first introduced the concept of eustress or good stress. Eustress is where you respond to a stressor such as a challenge with positive feelings because you feel it will bring you deeper fulfillment or personal satisfaction. When you are competing at sports, exercising, riding a roller coaster, watching a scary movie, or working on a project that has meaning to you . . . the stress that results is eustress. According to Selye's research, even under eustress, the stress hormones secreted can still have a degrading impact on the body.

In your most stressful moments, it can sometimes feel as if you are being pulled in a million directions emotionally, physically, mentally, spiritually, and in all the other aspects of your life. David Simon taught me a pithy definition of stress: *how we respond when our needs are not met.* And for most people, this occurs between eight and fifteen times each day. Here are just a few examples. You order what you think is the simplest dish on the menu, and it takes the longest to come out . . . and when it does, it's cold or not what you thought you ordered. A conversation doesn't go the way you planned. The phone rings, and it's him; the phone rings, and it's not him. Someone cuts you off on the highway. You have a one o'clock lunch date, and you rush to get there on time only to have to wait 30 minutes for your friend to arrive. You stub your toe. Your computer freezes up. Your TV show doesn't record. You're hoping to hear news that never arrives. You hear something else that makes you change your plans. You misspeak or do something that doesn't feel "right."

Each day we experience small disappointments and larger expectations not being met. You expect something to happen, and it doesn't; or it does but doesn't play out exactly as you had scripted it. Think about how many times a day *your* needs are not met.

Whenever your needs aren't met, you have the potential to respond in many ways. When you respond reflexively instead of reflectively—acting out a conditioned pattern or automatically arguing or withdrawing instead of choosing a more intuitive or enlightened response—you lower yourself to your most primitive state such as the fight-or-flight response, which is hardwired into your DNA.

It's not what happens to you but how you respond to life that determines your emotional and physical health. You can express your disappointment in many ways—from barking at someone to storming out of a discussion to rolling your eyes and taking a breath. But what happens to all these unmet needs . . . big and small? Each time your needs are not met and you react to this stress with disappointment, your heart beats faster, your breathing speeds up, your immune system shuts down, and your platelets get stickier. How long do you think this can go on before these primitive interpretations and reactions lead you to experience disease in your bodymind?

Over time, chronic stress can lead to emotional, physical or sexual dysfunction; increase your chances of getting sick; and may manifest as chronic illness such as irritable bowel syndrome, fibromyalgia, lupus, Crohn's disease, migraine headaches, and even skin disorders like psoriasis as well as panic attacks and palpitations.

Think of a current situation in which your needs are not getting met. Most likely this involves another person (or even yourself) who has disappointed you with a certain behavior or the lack of a behavior you desire.

Close your eyes, and see that person in your mind's eye. What feelings do you have for this individual? Why are you angry or disappointed? What did they do or not do? Maybe this person is you. Are you holding a grudge against yourself or someone else? Feel all the physical and emotional waves that flow through you when you put your attention on this person and this issue.

Since hopefully you're not facing a physical threat at this very moment, it would be impossible for your body-mind to invoke fight or flight in the physical sense. But you are capable of deploying an emotional fight-or-flight response called the *reactive* or *ego response.*

How we respond—essentially, what we do—with our feelings ultimately determines our emotional health. What are you doing with your feelings about the person you're thinking about? Repressing them and withdrawing? Holding on and strategically lashing out with resentment? Letting them drive your thoughts . . . building the drama? Consider the long-term consequences of not having your needs met and the toll it can take on you emotionally, psychologically, and physically. How long have you held on to this grievance?

Emotional Charge and the Ego Response

Since this nonphysical form of the fight-or-flight response is more emotionally based, we respond with emotional charge rather than punching someone or running away; we bark back or shut down. It's still a very primitive response, and we use it when our ego, rather than our life, is threatened. When our actual flesh is threatened, fight or flight kicks in; when our sense of self (our ego) is challenged, the ego response is the most common biological response. David Simon has referred to the ego response as "crossing the mine field." This is the realm of *I, me, mine*—our magnificent ego, our sense of self . . . our sense of ownership of people, things, and experiences. When that ownership is questioned or one of our boundaries is challenged or attacked, we lash out to defend it or shut down in resignation.

The ego response has the whole spectrum of fight or flight woven into its emotional expressions. The fight version of the ego response may manifest as reactive, angry, argumentative behavior. The flight version of the ego response can take the expression of emotionally shutting down or withdrawal, such as refusing to converse with another person or give only terse replies. More extreme forms of flight are expressed through non-nourishing escapist behaviors such as substance abuse, excessive television viewing, gambling, or Internet addiction.

Think of a time you were having a heated discussion and found yourself reacting with anger, raising your voice, or even barking at another person. And at some point, most of us have reacted with the emotional version of the flight response as we walked away, shut down dialogue, or hung up on someone. It's the classic "talk to the hand" directive of walking away from a conversation.

Men and women tend to deal with stressful situations differently. While this is a broad generalization and exceptions naturally exist, men are more likely to respond to an emergency or perceived threat with a more masculine response such as aggression (fight), while women are more likely to respond with the more feminine response of fleeing (flight). But because everyone has both masculine and feminine aspects, in any given moment, a man may flee a situation, while a woman might react with aggression. Recent studies have found that in addition to the fight-or-flight response, in a threatening situation, women are likely to use a third strategy, known as the befriend response, finding ways to defuse the crisis by enlisting cooperation. And in Twelve-Step programs and recovery circles, the freeze response (a form of flight) has emerged as a common withdrawal alternative to fight and flight.

The physiological and emotional responses to stress are well documented, and if we respond with an ego response to every need that's not met, we will certainly die sooner or live a more painful life. Fortunately, meditation offers us a tool that helps reverse the impact that fight-or-flight and ego responses have on our minds and bodies. Meditation is the tool that can unravel the cellular damage that stress has caused and alter our DNA hardwiring of the fight-or-flight response. Research by 2009 Nobel Prize winners Elizabeth H. Blackburn, Carol W. Greider, and Jack W. Szostak discovered that our chromosomes are protected by *telomeres* and the enzyme *telomerase*. These protective caps on the ends of the long, threadlike DNA molecules that carry our genes determine the very health of each cell as it is created. As lower levels of stress hormones are introduced into our system through a daily meditation practice, telomeres mend, and our immune function rises. Emotionally, we start to respond more intuitively and less reactively, releasing us from the prison of ego responses. In time, we will be moved from an existence of conditioned, limiting beliefs to a more unconditioned life, pregnant with infinite possibilities and better health.

The Restful Awareness Response

When we meditate, our body's chemistry changes. In fact, we experience the opposite of the physiological effects produced by the fight-or-flight and ego responses. We are less inclined to perspire, our breathing and heart rate slow, our body's production of stress hormones decreases, our sex hormone production increases, our growth hormone levels are elevated, our immune system strengthens, and our platelets become less sticky as blood flows more easily throughout our entire body. As these physiological shifts to our physical body occur, our mind calms, anxiety lessens, stress seems to shed, and there is an emotional shift in how we perceive unmet needs. This state of restful awareness can last for a moment or through the entire meditation. But the beauty of this process is that the state of restful awareness continues to benefit our bodies even after our meditation session. And as we meditate on a regular basis, we slowly and gently shift our automatic response mechanism to a more unconditioned one.

In the state of restful awareness, we move through situations with greater grace and ease. We are more reflective and less reflexive. We're less likely to lash out or have knee-jerk reactions, because we are not coming from a conditioned space. We're less impulsive and more intuitive. We're making more conscious choices, because we intuitively know what is the highest choice in that moment—the one that honors our Self and the person we are interacting with; the one that elevates both of us to the highest plane of existence; the one that comes from a heart filled with compassion, forgiveness, and a desire for peace.

In the state of restful awareness, we are more open to multiple interpretations of a situation or scenario. We become less attached to our previous interpretations, and our need to defend them feels less urgent. We see the bigger picture . . . a more expanded landscape . . . rather than the more narrow view we once had. Over the first few weeks of daily meditation, this grace, ease, and expanded awareness weave themselves intermittently through our interactions. As we continue to meditate and spend time in stillness and silence, each day becomes more comfortable; restful awareness becomes more and more our natural state; and greater clarity begins to unfold. It becomes less important to defend our point of view because we see greater possibilities, and creative solutions emerge to once-daunting challenges. Constrictions magically open up, and every moment becomes more expansive.

We become more alert, more creative, more intuitive, and more relaxed. We start having anxiety-free days, and stress becomes more manageable. And our first response to unmet needs is no longer the ego response . . . that's so *last week!*

Our more common response starts to be one of restful awareness—of silent witnessing before we act out old, conditioned response patterns yet again. This "new" state could also be called *restful alertness*, because our senses are heightened, and we begin to experience a new lightness of being. Little things don't irritate us or knock us off course as easily. We become more fluid in our thoughts and actions—more intuitive . . . then more creative . . . then more visionary . . . and then we start seeing miracles throughout every day.

Experiencing greater peace of mind throughout the day is also very common, as is more restful sleep, better digestion, and an entire new level of vitality. We are slowly returning to equilibrium—to wholeness!

Many of my students tell me that 30 minutes of meditation is more restorative to them than 30 minutes of sleep. If you have an irregular or abnormal sleep pattern, it can normalize in just a few days after you have gotten comfortable with your new meditation routine. Of course, if the thing that keeps you awake is a deeper emotional constriction or pain, meditation will help to relieve the acuteness of the pain. However, only a commitment to deeper self-discovery, emotional release, and emotional healing work will relieve the emotional pain at the core of your insomnia.

Releasing Stored Emotional Pain

To uncover, mobilize, and release this dormant, emotionally toxic plaque, I recommend a doctor-designed emotional healing process. Two programs with which I am intimately familiar are the Hoffman Institute's Quadrinity Process (which I attended in 2006), developed by Dr. Robert Hoffman, and the Chopra Center's Free to Love/Free to Heal process, created by Dr. David Simon. I was fortunate enough to work with David on the last few Free to Love workshops with fellow teacher Trista Thorp and for a while facilitated his process, in which we helped people identify their emotional pain, mobilize it, release it, and then heal their wounds. Essentially, deconstruct your emotional self and then reconstruct it with less baggage, less conditioning, and less anger. David was particularly brilliant in helping people see their story as an excuse for not making conscious choices in the present. Once you can step out of victim mode and take ownership of your life, you can write the next chapter in which you've chosen lightness over baggage, forgiveness over resentment, compassion over blame, and more conscious choices over conditioned ones. It's impossible to do this work and not feel a bit lighter, and that lightness only increases with a daily meditation practice.

I have found these emotional healing processes to be powerful pathways to forgiveness, compassion, real growth, and self-love. They allow you to experience a better version of yourself. This ongoing process of opening my constrictions and releasing them has taken my meditation practice to an even higher level, because I continue to become lighter, bringing less mental turbulence into my daily meditation sessions. In essence, lightening my load has unlocked a spiritual doorway for me that has expanded my understanding of meditation as a process of surrender. And that powerful energy of stillness then translates into my daily life. I no longer find it so necessary to try to be in control of every moment. Sometimes it's okay to set your course, engage your intention, lean in the direction of your desires, and let the universe do the driving.

Spiritual Benefits of Meditation

The spiritual aspect of meditation has long been misunderstood. Each of us is seeking a reconnection to the whole, to source, to one-ness. We each choose the most resonating path to understand and express the bigger, more profound, universal concepts of life, death, pain, love, truth, bliss, and purpose. Some people don't care about these things, because their awareness has not drifted into these concepts at this point in their life. Ultimately, each of us will walk through these experiences and then be faced with these questions. So even if someone is not currently engaged in this conversation, simply having an awareness of these natural principles of life invokes an understanding that there is something bigger, more expansive, more knowing, and more intelligent than we are. We could call that entity a universal being. Never born and never died. Existing in every moment and connected to all things simultaneously. Some of us call that God.

In Vedanta, the ancient Indian philosophy of self-realization, there is a school of thought known as *Advaita* (pronounced "add-vye-ta"), a Sanskrit term for "non-duality." According to Advaita, one-ness is the only reality. Everything else is an illusion, known in Sanskrit as *maya*. The philosophy states that our ignorance of our one-ness—which is also an illusion—is the cause for all suffering in the world. Only through the direct knowledge of this one-ness (actually experiencing it) can true liberation occur. In Sanskrit, this liberation is called *moksha* (*moke-sha*). Understanding that all of existence is non-dual—not two things but *one* pure whole—is the path to moksha.

Most of us grew up in homes where we were introduced to an all-knowing, all-seeing, infinite being known as God. How else can finite flesh beings such as us, with limited tools and a limited understanding, ingest such a beyond-this-realm concept as one-ness? There needs to be an almighty being that embodies all the characteristics of one-ness so we can better understand them—a sort of middleman between us and one-ness. Most of us have a similar understanding regarding our God's nature. Essentially this being created everything; controls or influences everything; is everywhere at once or has demi-gods or avatars who can be anywhere; is infinite, immortal, omnipresent, spans the existence of time and, therefore, is timeless; is capable of resurrection and rebirth; can be worshipped and appealed to; and has the ability to craft what we would consider miracles.

Even if you weren't brought up in a formal religious or spiritual tradition (if you are an atheist you can still meditate and receive all the benefits you are seeking) it is still likely that you believe there is some form of intelligence beyond ours. So whether your orientation is toward the divine, a god, multiple gods, or a higher power, we define our personal understanding of this universal nature as *spirituality. Essentially, spirituality is the journey we take in each moment from our most individual Self to our most universal Self and then back again. From constriction to expansion!*

When our mind analyzes this being or power, we see this omniscient, omnipotent, infinite God or spirit at once in everything and yet separate from us and the world. Advaita would say this separation exists only on the surface, only in our mind. Deeper below the surface, our mind, body, and spirit are all the same things—pure, unbounded consciousness—one-ness wearing different disguises. According to Vedanta, liberation lies in knowing the reality of this one-ness and experiencing spirit through varying aspects of study (*gyan*), devotion (*bhakti*), action (*karma*), and practice (*raja* or the royal path).

Two of the practices of the royal path that most directly connect us to spirit are meditation (restful awareness) and yoga (body-centered restful awareness). The path to this understanding of spirit is a deeper understanding of who we are, what we really want in life, and why we are here. This has been referred to as the expansion of consciousness—moving from a constricted, conditioned space where we identify and define ourselves as the roles we play in life and the things we own (essentially, our positions and our possessions) to the more expansive perspective of who we are, how we are connected to everything, and what we came here to do.

Discovering Our True Self

Most people embarking on a new meditation practice do so because they are seeking more from life or more from themselves. As they begin to explore their thoughts, dreams, and daily choices, an awareness settles in that they are not their thoughts or their body, but that they are more than that—they are pure, unbounded consciousness sealed in a flesh casing for the span of a lifetime. That perspective changes everything, because it means that in any moment, anything is possible. Our previous patterns, ruts, roadblocks, conditioned responses, thoughts, and behaviors start becoming less conditioned as they are bathed in droplets of our unconditioned Self.

The purest, most defenseless and unconditioned aspects of ourselves begin to take hold in our daily routine and then they weave themselves into our physiology. With each meditation, you move ever deeper into the most universal, infinite facets of your being . . . those at your very core: your unbounded, unconditioned Self.

As you continue to meditate, your very foundation expands. And if your starting point for all things is already at a higher level, everything that flows from that point on vibrates at a higher frequency. You see the world differently; you experience your life with fuller grace and greater ease. You recognize that everything is Spirit—and we are all connected. Each of us is a wave in a vast ocean that contains billions of waves, that vast one-ness from which we occasionally pop up to individuate ourselves, and, after a few moments, collapse back into the one-ness of the unified surf.

I believe that one of the biggest reasons meditation is not more prevalent is because it's impossible to convey the transformational nature of the practice. People try it and if they don't have an aha! moment or achieve enlightenment in a week, they abandon the practice. Osho, the great philosopher and guru, is known to have said, "Enlightenment is finding that there is nothing to find. Enlightenment is to come to know that there is nowhere to go." You don't need to be a guru, yogi, or believer in any one philosophy or religion to incorporate this capability into your life. You just need the willingness to try it. So what's the best path? In the next few chapters, we explore a variety of meditation practices from traditions throughout time and cultures throughout the world. As you practice each one, see what resonates most, practice it, and live the benefits!

PART II

MANY PATHS TO ONE-NESS

There are thousands of schools and philosophies of meditation. And every school of meditation has its unique technique or way of helping you to experience present-moment awareness. I celebrate them all, and this book honors every tool, technology, and body of knowledge that can help you quiet the fluctuations of the mind and achieve deeper meaning, purpose, peace, and fulfillment in your life. I personally have explored many different schools of meditation, and I've practiced several for as little as two months to as long as 15 years. Since 2002, I have practiced Primordial Sound Meditation, usually two times a day for 30 minutes and sometimes more, if I am teaching a class or leading a retreat that day.

At the height of its popularity, the Chopra Center's Seduction of Spirit weeklong meditation retreat often contained four meditations each day, starting with a sunrise meditation for the bold early risers (some of these on Florida's talcum beaches, amid Sedona's Red Rocks, on La Costa's misty lawns, and high in the majestic peaks of Whistler are etched into my soul forever). Throughout the past decade, Deepak and David would teach at these workshops, and I had the privilege of leading the meditations. There's something very powerful in meditating with 450 of our closest meditating friends in a series of 30-minute meditation sessions known as "rounds."

The concept of rounding is practiced in many meditation retreats. You meditate in rounds of 30 minutes and then stop and bring your attention back into your body through yoga, breathwork, or dance. Then, at the peak of your activity, you stop, settle in, and go back in for another 30 minutes of meditation. At my very first retreat, the rounding went on for hours each day for seven whole days, interspersed with advanced meditation techniques known as sutras and energy work. For days, this realm of stillness and silence permeates everything you do—from washing your face to practicing yoga to chewing your food to interacting with other people. Just imagine what it's like when all the activity you thought was so critical to your existence is replaced by stillness and quietude.

After several days of this level of practice, you experience the layers of your conditioned Self begin to peel away. By spending hours in the stillness and silence of your own purest essence, you come closer than you ever have to experiencing your own soul. And then you realize that everyone around you is going through the same thing, peeling away layers of this conditioned life to reveal their true, unconditioned essence. This experience is described in spiritual circles as being "naked"—when all the layers of your conditioned life have been peeled away and nothing but your soul remains.

The combination of daily yoga, meditation, group meals, energy work, dancing, lectures on the soul, teachings from the Vedas, and group interaction interweaves the physical, emotional, and spiritual components of meditation into a very personal journey, traveling from your most ego-based, individual self to the most divine and cosmic aspects of your universal Self. I encourage you, when the time is right (and you will know when that is), to treat yourself to a meditation retreat. Whether you attend Seduction of Spirit, or find another weeklong meditation retreat, spending that much time in stillness will transform every cell in your body.

You may never attend a meditation retreat, but you have the ability to receive the same benefits by living this experience each day with a simple meditation practice. The key is to *do* it rather than try to figure it out intellectually. The Third Zen Patriarch, Jianzhi Sengcan, also known as Seng-t'san, confirmed this in his Zen poem *Xinxin Ming (Hsin Hsin Ming):* "The more you talk and think about it, the further astray you wander from the truth. Stop talking and thinking, and there is nothing you will not be able to know. To return to the root is to find the meaning, but to pursue appearances is to miss their source. At the moment of inner enlightenment there is a going beyond appearance and emptiness."

These words may sound New Agey, but he wrote them 1,500 years ago. And if you think about it, very few moments in our lives go by in total stillness and silence. In virtually every moment of your life, whether you are sleeping, dreaming, or awake, you are in activity. Even when you have the chance to be in stillness and silence, such as when you first walk through your front door or when you sit down in your car, most likely you choose activity.

How long does it take before you reach for your iPod, turn on a TV, listen to the radio, speak, hum, sing, eat, read, rock your leg, tap your finger, lick your lips, make a call, text someone, get online, connect with another being, or stretch your body? These are all expressions of activity, and you stay in activity until your bodymind collapses at night in sleep in order to rejuvenate.

When you are in a deep state of rest, when you are sleeping or dreaming, these are known as dull states—states of restful dullness. There is still activity in every moment of dreaming sleep: rapid eye movements, physical experiences emanating from the depths of your dreams. And in deep sleep, when there is stillness, it is not the alert stillness you experience when you are in meditation; it is dull stillness.

Of all the practices and behaviors I have explored, meditation is the easiest and most effective one you can engage in to experience present-moment witnessing awareness in a state of stillness and silence—pure restful awareness in an alert state—and ultimately, unity of your physical self, your emotional and egoistic self, and your spiritual Self.

There is only one stillness and silence that rests within you, there is only one universal force that flows through everything, and there is only one present moment. Yet there are so many ways to access it and become aware of it—contemplative prayer, physical forms of meditation that use the senses, and communing with nature. There are walking, dancing, lovemaking . . . and even smoking meditations popularized by Osho.

The chapters in **Part II: Many Paths to One-ness** walk you through the most common techniques and accessible practices so that you can get a sense of what each feels like and gravitate toward the one that most resonates with you. I have explored all of the following meditations, ultimately finding Primordial Sound Meditation to be the easiest to ritualize on a daily basis and therefore the most powerful practice for me. However, it took me many years of serial meditating . . . dabbling, immersing, stopping, starting again, being distracted, immersing again, stopping, using meditation to cope with crisis, starting again, and stopping a third time before I finally arrived at making Primordial Sound Meditation part of my daily routine. I'm hoping to help you arrive at your own practice less circuitously.

When most people think of meditation, they picture someone chanting "Om" either out loud or silently. This practice is known as mantra meditation, and I'll go more deeply into that form of meditation a bit further on up the road. But first, join me as I share my own meditation journey with you and the many forms that I have been fortunate to experience over my meditating lifetime. Some may resonate with you more than others; some may be more practical for you to practice than others. Yet recognizing the various ways to quiet the fluctuations of the mind to achieve stillness and silence in your life can be an amazing gift that will connect you more deeply to this precious existence of ours on planet Earth.

CHAPTER FOUR

SECRETS OF BODYMIND MEDITATION

*"A moment. The moment of orgasm. The moment
by the ocean when there is just the wave.
The moment of being in love. The moment of crisis
when we forget ourselves and do just what is needed."*

— RAM DASS

Let's begin with one of the easiest and most scientifically sound meditation techniques and the one that first got me hooked on meditation as a valuable life tool: *biofeedback*. Biofeedback is the process of becoming aware of various physiological functions by monitoring them so that you can influence, alter, and/or control them. Over time, you can train your sympathetic nervous system to be less reactive to stressors and to recover from them more quickly. Through the practice of biofeedback, you can influence your pulse rate, breath, muscles, brain waves, your perception of pain, and other bodily functions.

You observe your progress on a computer monitor, and as you get closer to your targeted pulse variance, breathing flow, and brain wave frequency, you see the changes on the screen—hence the word *feedback*. Biofeedback is used to manage stress, lessen anxiety, regulate blood pressure, improve physical performance, ease headaches, and heighten mental acuity.

Early in my meditation journey, I enrolled in a research study to explore the mind-body connection. It focused on measuring and monitoring my biosignals as I performed various behaviors to lower them. Biosignals are the electric currents produced across a group of cells, a specific tissue, or an organ such as the brain, heart, or skin. Energy runs through us and so do measurable amounts of electricity and magnetic pull. Modern science has even observed and measured the electrical currents and biosignals that plants generate. The goal of biofeedback is to monitor your biosignals so closely that you can adjust and alter them as they are occurring.

You can do it right now. Instead of breathing regularly, right now inhale very slowly through your nose to the count of four.

One. Two. Three. Four.

Hold this in to the count of four.

And now exhale through your nostrils to the count of four.

Now hold that out to the count of four.

Continue this process eight more times. This should take you about a minute and a half. I'll wait.

Most likely you've slowed your breathing to less than ten breaths per minute, slowed your pulse by 20 percent, lessened your anxiety in this moment, and reduced the moisture that your skin exudes when you are overexcited or stressed. You are calmer now than you were only two minutes ago. If we chose to, any of us could formally monitor these biosignals to track our progress. The traditional biosignals monitored in biofeedback are the EKG (electrocardiogram), EEG (electroencephalogram), HRV (heart-rate variability), and the GSR (galvanic skin response). The HRV measures the time or interval between each beat of your heart. Strangely enough, variation in the beat-to-beat interval is the sign of a healthy heart. Infinite possibilities even in your heartbeat! The GSR detects increased levels of perspiration generated by our autonomic nervous system and is used in traditional lie detection processes when one is hooked up to a polygraph. In addition to becoming more conductive during the telling of a lie, our skin also perspires when we experience anger, fear, pain, surprise, sexual feelings, and emotional arousal. The use of lie detector tests in court cases remains questionable, but the truth about lie detectors is that they do reveal certain involuntary responses to stressful situations, such as increased skin conductivity and breathing rhythms. But they don't mean that someone is lying . . . just showing stress.

The Body Never Lies

In every moment, our biosignals reveal our true emotional state, yet very few people around us can see them. Our mind sends signals to our body, which then reacts spontaneously, creating the perfect feedback loop. We wear our emotions on our bodies and ultimately in our bodies. David Simon has said that 90 percent of our physical toxicity is emotionally derived. There are even those who specialize in the study of human emotions by interpreting facial expressions. One of those is Dr. Paul Ekman, a psychologist who can determine with near certainty whether a person is lying based on small visual clues known as microexpressions. Ekman established that the face has 43 distinct and involuntary muscle movements that create thousands of expressions, including the seven basic human emotions of anger, contempt, disgust, fear, happiness, sadness, and surprise. It was Ekman's work that was the inspiration for the TV show *Lie to Me,* starring Tim Roth as the microexpression expert Dr. Cal Lightman. This level of research and understanding was in its infancy when I entered the biofeedback study many years ago. It was a six-month study that had fairly rigorous controls, especially for a second-year college student—no alcohol, no drugs of any kind, and no mind-altering substances for half a year! Weekly blood and urine tests kept the participants true to the process. And every other day for six months, I visited the clinic for 90 minutes, first slowing down for a half hour to establish a baseline and then plugging into an EKG through a skin-conductivity cuff with ten rubber finger thimbles that connected my internal electrical circuit board to the computer's motherboard for an hour.

In front of three lab techs in white coats with clipboards, I performed exercise after exercise, using my mind, my breath, and my heart. I stared into a dashboard that integrated several monitors and dials, including one that showed me my blood pressure. I learned to lower the numbers on command, starting with a basic BP reading of 160/120. Within a few months, I dropped it down to

100/60, which is about where my blood pressure reading has stayed for the past 20 years.

As the months passed and we approached the end of the study, I had to proactively increase my resting pulse after it plummeted below 50 beats a minute for a few weeks. I found myself becoming lightheaded in elevators and airplanes. To regain my equilibrium, I began to secretly reverse my intentions during each day's testing, and all my numbers began to rise, making me look like an unsuccessful test subject. I ultimately revealed to the clinicians that biofeedback worked so effectively that I had to elevate my blood pressure to keep from passing out.

They kicked me out of the study!

Exploring the HeartMath Technique

In recent years, I have practiced biofeedback using a program developed by the Institute of HeartMath, in which you attach sensors to your fingers and breathe in various depths and frequencies to create what's known as coherence—a highly efficient physiological state in which your nervous, cardiovascular, hormonal, and immune systems are all entrained and working together in a balanced and harmonious state. The state of coherence is very similar to what athletes refer to as being in "the zone." Everything is in total alignment, but most strikingly, it happens with effortless ease.

In the HeartMath program I used, the process started with a black-and-white picture on the screen that slowly transformed into color as I achieved deeper and deeper states of relaxation. As I went deeper into a state of coherence, more vivid and colorful aspects of nature emerged from the background—a waterfall, a rainbow, bunnies, and deer prancing through lush, green forests that transformed from monochromatic to Technicolor. The more I got into the zone, the more the colors flowed. This positive reinforcement subliminally helps you lower all of your activity levels while you are in a state of rest.

Biofeedback's Continuing Evolution

Over the last few years, as technology has advanced, biofeedback monitors and feedback mechanisms have become affordable and almost gamelike in their look and feel. They have entered the mainstream meditation world marketed primarily as stress management tools. Biofeedback has evolved to include more brainwave monitoring using sensors attached to the scalp. Advanced computer software now allows people to see their brainwaves and, through training and practice, change their brainwave patterns to improve their physical, cognitive, and emotional health through a similar process known as neurofeedback.

Deepak Chopra has consistently been on the forefront of merging new technologies with ancient teachings. In his quest to bring this timeless body of knowledge to a younger generation, he created the *Leela* interactive gaming experience for Xbox360, which uses movement and breath to help you connect to your energy centers. And years earlier, as the youngest gamers were just logging on to their first gaming experience, Deepak offered an alternative to the joystick-as-gun offerings with his groundbreaking *Journey to the Wild Divine*, in which you plugged your fingers into sleeves and used your pulse and breath to maneuver through real-life situations in a fantasy world.

Although I enjoyed the practice of biofeedback, and it garnered powerful physiological results, I found it to be a highly physical form of meditation that kept my body and mind very busy. You pay attention to the results of your breathing and meditating while it's actually happening, and I was always focused on seeing how much I was moving the dials. Although biofeedback slowed my breathing and my heart rate, and I ultimately dropped my resting pulse rate down to 45 beats per minute, I was never really in stillness. Silence, perhaps, but no stillness. I accomplished deep states of relaxation during my sessions, but it did not take me to that place of stillness and silence that I visit so easily using more subtle, less physical forms of meditation. It also never connected me to the experience of one-ness. I was more relaxed, more clearheaded, and had less stress in my life, but I still found myself passing out in elevators. So I searched for another meditation technique that wasn't so physical and active.

Bodymind meditations can help you relax and lower your blood pressure.

CHAPTER FIVE

SECRETS OF
VISUAL MEDITATION

---

*"Sometimes I think all my pictures are just pictures of me.
My concern is . . . the human predicament; only what I
consider the human predicament may simply be my own."*

— RICHARD AVEDON

In my early 20s, I met a woman who was really into candles—
an innocent pioneer in the realm of natural candle-making, which
is now a global, multibillion-dollar business. She had developed a
recipe with a soy base that contained essential aromatic oils, and
as the wicks burned, they unleashed a magnificent primal aroma
that awakened and healed. At times, she ringed her entire house
in row upon row of these intoxicating candles, and we would sit
in the dark and stare at the hundreds of flickering golden dancers
that surrounded us. We did this for as long as the candles burned—
sometimes with music playing and sometimes just sitting in stillness . . . in silence. The hypnotic attraction of the flames would
ultimately pull me in, and I would feel a sort of high as I floated
into the light and eventually merged with light itself, feeling my
body become porous and my individuality unfold into something
bigger than me . . . beyond me . . . everything and nothing at once,
BEing the moment.

It was years later, in an Ashtanga Vinyasa yoga class, that I
first was taught to use this focusing technique as part of the yoga
asana or pose. The technique was called *drishti* (also spelled *dristi*),
and in Sanskrit, it means "insight, wisdom, intelligence, or point
of view." During yoga practice, the drishti serves both as a way to
move beyond this local realm of space and time—beyond your

normal vision, beyond physical balance and equilibrium—and as a metaphor for focusing consciousness toward a vision of one-ness. It's a form of meditation in itself.

Drishti Meditation

When using a drishti during yoga practice or open-eyed meditation, you softly focus your gaze at some concentrated point while keeping your attention directed within. The drishti point can be a candle flame or the edge of your nostril, your third eye (the point between your eyebrows), your navel, or some point in the distance. Drishti isn't about the external object you are focusing on; the purpose is to draw your consciousness away from the distractions around you to a single focal point—a point from which your concentration is ultimately directed inward. In yoga practice, drishti is a point of focus where the gaze rests during poses of flexibility, balance, or strength. Focusing on a drishti aids concentration, since it is easier to become distracted when the eyes wander all over the room. In certain styles of yoga, each asana has a specific drishti, which also aids in alignment. For instance, in the yoga asana called *parvatasana,* also known as mountain pose or downward facing dog, your legs and arms create an A-frame, with your butt sticking high in the air, pulling up to the sky, and the drishti is your navel. In the yoga asana called *utthita parsvakonasana,* or extended side angle pose, you lean to the side, with one hand on the ground supporting you, and your drishti is upward toward your other hand, which is raised and extended, guiding your head up to the sky. You look to your raised fingers which ultimately become the sky which ultimately become one-ness.

It was legendary teacher and yogi Sri K. Pattabhi Jois who first introduced the soft-gaze drishti practice to the Western yoga world 70 years ago, teaching students to direct their awareness to one of nine points of focus on the physical body as they moved through the 28 asanas or poses of the practice. The ashtanga yoga tradition, popularized in America by guru Jois, describes nine classic drishtis and emphasizes a fixed gaze with soft eyes. They are:

1. Tip of the nose
2. Third eye
3. Navel
4. Thumbs
5. Hands
6. Big toes
7. Far to the right
8. Far to the left
9. Up to the sky

Let's experience these drishtis right now.

Take a deep breath in, hold it for a few beats, and then slowly let it out through your nostrils. Keep breathing at this same pace. Long, slow, deep inhales.

After you've done this a few times, drift your gaze to the tip of your nose. Feel your eyes cross and relax. Do this for a minute or so.

Now bring your awareness up to your third eye, located in the middle of your forehead, a bit above your eyebrows. Feel your eyes open and close. Stay in this space for a few minutes.

Now bring your attention to your navel. Look within. Keep your eyes in a soft gaze. Stay here for a few moments.

And now gently drift to your thumbs—no thoughts but your gaze for a few moments.

And now expand your awareness to include your whole hand. Remember to keep breathing . . . long . . . slow . . . deep breaths.

Now drift your gaze to your big toes. Wiggle them to bridge the energetic distance between your physical and astral toes.

Now without moving your head, drift your gaze all the way to the right, almost trying to see your right ear. Keep your gaze soft, and keep breathing.

Now move your eyes as far as they will gaze to the left.

After you've gazed left for a minute or so, bring the gaze to center, and raise your eyes up to the sky.

When you've done that for a minute or so, close your eyes, and just sit and let that process settle in.

How do you feel? Any different?

As with many forms of meditation, drishti meditation involves deep focus and concentration. In contrast, in the practice of Primordial Sound Meditation, one does not focus or concentrate, which personally, I found liberating. But focus and concentration can be powerful tools in yoga practice, because they allow you to move beyond your physical body to the drishti. And when you are in a state of body-centered restful awareness, the drishti ultimately becomes you . . . beyond space and time. It's a beautiful and deeply centering and unifying experience.

Sri Yantra Meditation

Similar to the act of drishti, *sri yantra* is another popular form of visual meditation. It is rooted in India's Vedic and yogic traditions.

For thousands of years, people have meditated by staring into the devotional labyrinths of Buddhist mandalas and Hindu yantras in order to achieve higher states of consciousness. These are visual representations of the journey of evolution, usually depicting a deity in the center that acts as the source of one-ness. Around the deity are ever-opening concentric circles (*mandala* is a Sanskrit term meaning "circle"), other geometric shapes, and depictions of nature or holy scenes.

The sri yantra took this devotional art to a new level in the eighth century as one of the first nonreligious geometric depictions of this sacred journey. *Sri* (also spelled *shri* and pronounced "shree") is Sanskrit for "wealth" or "abundance"; in this case it means "most revered." *Yantra* is a Sanskrit word for "vehicle" or "instrument." So the sri yantra is a revered visual instrument that uses the mathematical proportions known as the golden ratio. The scientific proportions used to create such structures as the Parthenon and the Great Pyramid at Giza are based on the same naturally occurring sacred ratios we witness in the development of pine cones, ferns, succulents, and nautilus shells. The sacred geometrics of the sri yantra depict a pure visual expression of the journey of existence, expanding from the cosmic one-ness (the source) to multiplicity (our personal expression of the universe) and then back to one-ness —all the while providing that very experience of one-ness. It is a meditation in itself.

Using what is now referred to as mathematical psychology, the ancient artisans of the sri yantra applied such scientific techniques as the Fibonacci sequence, which is the mathematical representation of the sacred ratio. The simultaneously static and dynamic interplay of all the elements of the sri yantra—squares, circles, "perfect" triangles, lines, and a point—depict the process of evolution (growth away from the source) and involution (coming from multiple layers back to one single source) in the form of a visual meditation. It has often been referred to as a visual representation of the vibration Om (said to include all the vibrational tones of the planet) and honors the power of masculine and feminine energy rather than the figure of a god or goddess.

Because it is a visual representation of the vibration Om, the sri yantra is considered the most powerful yantra for meditation for the fact that, first and foremost, it is a silent vibration—the unstruck bell! And that silent focus on the object of your attention disconnects you from all other activity and takes you on a journey into one-ness, where all your desires will be fulfilled. Meditating on the sri yantra is essentially a visual interplay and fusion of duality—the manifest world of form and phenomena, with non-duality—the formless unboundedness of the unmanifest world.

The sri yantra is formed by nine interlocking triangles that surround and radiate out from the central point that then creates 34 individual triangles. This centering point or dot, known as the *bindu,* is the junction point between the physical realm and its unmanifest source and represents the universe in all its abundance. Four of the larger triangles point upward, representing Shiva, or masculine energy. Five of the triangles point downward, representing Shakti, or feminine energy. Thus the sri yantra also represents the union of masculine and feminine divine energy.

Since the sri yantra is composed of nine triangles, it is often known as the *navayoni chakra* (*nava* means "nine," and *yoni* refers to female womb as the source of all life, and *chakra* means "energy center"). Together, the nine triangles are interlaced in such a way as to form 43 smaller triangles in a web representative of the entire cosmos or a womb symbolic of creation. This is surrounded by a lotus of 8 petals, a lotus of 16 petals, and an earth square resembling a temple with four doors that face all four sides representing north, south, east, and west.

The sri yantra is also known as the *nava chakra* because it can also be seen as having nine levels. These levels, displayed in all traditional sri yantras, start from the center and radiate outward from:

1. *Sarva Anandamaya,* composed of a point or bindu

2. *Sarva Siddhi prada,* composed of 1 small triangle

3. *Sarva Rogahara,* composed of 8 small triangles

4. *Sarva Rakshakara,* composed of 10 small triangles

5. *Sarva Arthasadhaka,* composed of 10 small triangles

6. *Sarva Saubhagyadayaka,* composed of 14 small triangles

7. *Sarva Sankshobahana,* a circle comprising an 8-petal lotus

8. *Sarva Aasa Paripuraka,* a circle comprising a 16-petal lotus

9. *Trilokya Mohana* or *Bhupara,* comprising a square of 3 lines with 4 portals

To perform a sri yantra meditation, sit down comfortably at a table or desk. Prop up the yantra one to two feet away, directly in front of your gaze, or watch it on a monitor. (Visit the meditation resources page at **davidji.com** for a full-page, full-color sri yantra.)

Once you are comfortably set in front of your sri yantra, read the directions below and feel free to gaze at the image on the page.

As you look at the yantra, allow your eyes to focus on its center. This dot in the center is called the bindu, which represents the unity that underlies all the diversity of the physical world. Now allow your eyes to see the triangle that encloses the bindu. The downward-pointing triangle represents the feminine creative power, the womb of all creation, while the upward-facing triangle represents male energy, movement, and transformation. Allow your vision to expand to include the circles outside of the triangles. They represent the cycles of cosmic rhythms. The image of the circle embodies the notion that time has no beginning and no end. The farthest region of space and the innermost nucleus of an atom both pulsate with the same rhythmic energy of creation. That rhythm is within you and without you.

Bring your awareness to the lotus petals outside the circle. Notice that they are pointing outward, as if opening. They illustrate the unfolding of our understanding. The lotus also represents the heart, the seat of the Self. When the heart opens, understanding comes.

The square at the outside of the yantra represents the world of form, the material world that our senses show us, the illusion of separateness, well-defined edges, and boundaries. At the periphery of the figure are four T-shaped portals, or gateways. Notice that they point toward the interior of the yantra, the inner spaces of life. They represent our earthly passage from the external and material to the internal and sacred.

Now take a moment to gaze into the yantra, and as if in slow motion, let the different shapes and patterns emerge naturally, allowing your eyes to be held loosely in focus. Gaze at the center of the yantra. You are gazing on perfection: the golden ratio. Pure balance and equilibrium. Let's drink it in. Without moving your eyes, gradually and very slowly begin to expand your field of vision, lingering over each layer as you expand your vision. Continue slowly expanding your vision until you are taking in information from greater than 180 degrees.

Notice that all this information was there all along, but because you were fully present, you *just* became aware of it as it unfolded. This is akin to the unfolding of your life's journey . . . from the one source to individuation, ever evolving, changing, shifting, transforming, and moving outward in so many different directions.

Now slowly reverse the process by gently drawing your attention back in. Slowly move from taking in everything around you, and begin to narrow your gaze. Move your awareness slowly back to the yantra's four gates, and stay there for a few moments. Then ever so gently, move deeper into the yantra. Drift your soft gaze slowly back through each circular channel of lotus petals and triangles and ultimately back to the bindu—back to the source. Take a few minutes to do this.

This process of moving back to the bindu is called "involution"—moving from multiplicity, our multidimensionality, to one-ness as you drift your awareness back into the center of the yantra, layer by layer.

Don't feel the need to stare at the yantra beyond a comfortable amount of time; from 5 to 15 minutes is perfectly acceptable, there is no need to overdo it. Whatever length of time *you* are comfortable with should work. And now go through the process of evolution and involution.

After you have gazed at the yantra for a few minutes, gently close your eyes for between 5 and 25 minutes, and let the yantra unfold in your mind's eye. This practice of letting the yantra unfold within you is a powerful part of the meditation, as the stored geometric images drift you back and forth between DOing and BEing. The patterns of creativity represented by these primordial shapes express the fundamental forces of nature that flow through existence and through you. When you are done with both parts of the meditation, feel free to simply sit and slowly let the subtle nature of what you just experienced ripple through your thoughts, your being, and your breath. Notice how you feel. Notice the volume and the activity levels of the world around you and then become aware of the world within you. Just witness yourself through the whole process. And breathe.

Always remember to be gentle with yourself, and take a few minutes (or longer if possible) to sit quietly before you resume physical activity. The trancelike effect of the sri yantra meditation can carry over into the next few hours of your day, so make sure not to drive or operate heavy equipment immediately following this or any form of meditation.

After practicing yantra meditations, you will lose the feeling of separation between the yantra and your Self, essentially disconnecting from the concept of separateness itself. You will experience one-ness when you cannot differentiate whether you are in the yantra or the yantra is in you. *Note:* Doing the meditation isn't going to put you in a permanent state of psychosis, make you unable to distinguish boundaries, or unable to live in the daily world.

The yantra meditation is not meant to replace your daily practice but can be inserted at any point in your day. It will act as a complementary practice to whatever other form of meditation you are engaged in. Drishti meditations are powerful experiences and can help progressively slow the fluctuations of the mind, while providing glimpses of spiritual awakening. Yet receiving visual images and activating your powers of focus are still *activities* that keep one rooted in the physical and subtle realms of activity! So let's keep exploring other forms of meditation so you can taste even more subtle experiences.

Visual meditations can help you concentrate and focus.

CHAPTER SIX

SECRETS OF SOUND MEDITATION

"Why are there trees I never walk under but large and melodious thoughts descend upon me?"

— WALT WHITMAN

Every life form on this planet expresses itself through sound. Every animal has a distinct voice—from the basso profundo rumblings of elephants and the full-mouthed roars of the big cats to the squeals and caws of finches and exotic parrots. Gargantuan whales and their smaller dolphin cousins ripple their magnificent songs through the depths of the sea, while mice squeak, lizards hiss, weasels whimper, owls hoot, and wolves howl to each other across the miles.

Sound can bring us to the present moment. It can also drift us into the past and sometimes even into the future for short bursts of time. The world around us calls out in myriad voices: the ocean churns and shouts even as it caressingly laps at the shore; trees creak and moan as they bend and sway in the gusting wind, their branches shaking their leaves like maracas; fields of flowers sing in unison; even the thousands of blades of grass in every front yard and backyard bow and reach for the sky as they subtly chant their whispering chorus.

Every plant and animal on earth uses sound to connect. The whole planet is in song, and hearing it is simply a question of the tool we use to listen—our ears, our eyes, our hearts, our skin, our bones, our minds, our souls. When we can elevate a particular sound until it is the loudest vibration in our awareness, that can become our meditation. It can be the sound of human voices singing, chanting, or speaking; the emanations of metal or crystal bowls; the chiming of cymbals and gongs; or the imperceptible echoes of sound waves. All can be a form of meditation. But just as the sri yantra meditation is not meant to be a replacement for your daily meditation practice, sound and guided meditations are meant to be a complement to your daily practice.

Guided Meditation

I love guided meditations. I have experienced deep healing and powerful aha! moments listening to guided meditations. Some can be effective in helping you train your mind and body. Many athletes use guided visualizations to reinforce and fine-tune an experience they would like to replicate, such as hitting the perfect golf drive, dunking a basketball, kicking a field goal, or swinging a hockey stick just before the puck arrives. By picturing the process and desired outcome over and over in your mind, you become primed for when the event actually takes place, such as timing the swing of a bat to an oncoming fastball heading at you at 100 miles per hour.

Less popularized are the meditations and visualizations for nonathletic activities, such as relaxing the body before an MRI, releasing stress before and during a plane flight or medical procedure, preparing for a difficult conversation, lessening and releasing physical pain stored within the body, practicing a presentation, and doing deeper emotional work to release experiences that no longer serve you.

I've developed several guided meditations that bring you into the present moment by taking you out of your past, out of your future, and out of your head by using words, sound, and music to take you on a journey of empowerment, acceptance, emotional healing, or peace. *Come Fly With Me,* my CD on stress-free flying, was birthed after several of my students revealed that they were horrified to fly on airplanes and were in emotional pain in the days and weeks leading up to the flight—from packing to checking in to boarding and especially during takeoff and landing. Now they, along with tens of thousands of airplane passengers, have a tool to help them move through these constrictions without the emotional turbulence.

Throughout the years—starting when I received a bootleg audio copy of Ram Dass reading passages from *Be Here Now,* to my freshman immersion into Zen philosophy, when Alan Watts guided me through a journey from my head to my soul—I have experienced powerful breakthroughs and expansions of awareness through guided meditations.

My deepest past-life regression was a guided meditation that Deepak led me through at a meditation retreat. It only lasted an hour, but it felt like centuries had shifted as he took me back to yesterday, and then last week, and then last month, last year, 10 years ago, 20 years ago, into the womb, and then beyond the womb into my previous life!

It was unbelievably transformative. And yes, I had drifted away to someplace in the ether. But it was not a meditation of stillness and silence. My hearing was activated; I was very subtly paying attention to the meaning of his words. My intellect was processing his utterances. My mind was engaged. I crafted my thoughts as he spoke. I was fully present yet immersed in activity. It felt a bit like sleepwalking. As long as we are listening, we are consciously activating attention and intention and maintaining a foot in the realm of activity—the realm of the conditioned world.

Depending on what you need at a particular moment in time, guided meditation can move you, open you, ready you, soothe you, or heal you. But it cannot replace the extended periods of time you spend in *unguided* meditation, where you enter the realm of no thought and into the stillness and silence that rests within.

It's a powerful starting point for those who want more peace and relaxation or less anxiety and stress. And so many of us came to meditation first through a guided meditation, because it's such a gentle way for first-timers to test the waters and experience some of meditation's many benefits without being frightened away by concepts of spirituality, mantra, or extended sitting "doing nothing."

So many of my students with strong and consistent mantra practices began their journey by hearing a guided meditation in a yoga class, on a CD, a download, or on their iPhone!

I have written and recorded hundreds of guided meditations, and many can be found online at **davidji.com, cdbaby.com,** iTunes, **amazon.com, chopra.com,** my YouTube channel, and various other websites. Just do an Internet search for "davidji guided meditations" to find the one that most resonates with you at the moment. I've also developed a free online meditation resource center for the readers of this book, which includes videos, downloads, tips, and additional meditation tools. To tap into these resources, including special guided meditations, visit **davidji.com** and enter the password **SECRETS.**

WHEN TO USE GUIDED MEDITATIONS

If you have a dedicated meditation practice, any other meditative or spiritual practice, included guided meditations, will be heightened by the power of you spending time each day in stillness and silence, so use your daily practice to complement any other guided, energy, or silent meditation you wish to add to your day. I recommend to my students that they meditate twice each day, following their breath or using a mantra such as their Primordial Sound (see Chapter 10) once in the morning upon waking and again in the afternoon or early evening. Between these sessions, they can use other meditation forms they desire, such as a daily guided meditation session, a midday pranayam or breathing session, or an evening chakra tuning before bed.

In Chapter 14, we'll go deeper into how to ground your daily practice and create an effortless meditation ritual.

Remember, the power of any other meditation you do rests on the consistency and frequency of your daily meditation practice—the bookends of your day.

The Sound of Bowls

Beyond the sound of the human voice speaking words with all their meaning and our conditioned associations, nonvocal vibrations can be even more powerful objects of attention in meditation. They also have an energetic aligning power as they flow through every cell of your body. Since the time of Buddha, practitioners have used gongs, chimes, crystal bowls, metal bowls, drums, and other natural vibrations to induce states of transformation and meditation, essentially using sound to take you into stillness.

The most enduring vibration creators are the bowls of Tibet and Nepal, which are traditionally made of an alloy known as *pancha dhatu* (meaning "five tissues or layers") or *panchaloha* (meaning "five metals"), a combination of copper, tin, zinc, iron, and a precious metal (usually either gold or silver). The craftspeople who make five-metal bowls especially cherish iron from meteorites.

To "play" a bowl, a padded mallet is tapped on the lip, edge, or side of the bowl; then in a clockwise direction, the mallet is ever so gently rubbed in a wandlike fashion around the outside of the bowl—like stirring a pot of soup (except on the outside)—to tease out the single vibration into a chorus of harmonies. Tibetan metal bowl masters place an "orchestra" of bowls in front them and move around the floor tapping, stirring, blowing into the bowls, gonging, and coaxing waves of vibrations into a powerful healing symphony.

The power of these multiple-metal blends lies in the fact that each metallic compound vibrates at a different speed, creating multiple harmonies and polyphonic waves of sound that ripple through your body. Other metal percussion instruments—such as cymbals, tingshas, gongs, and chimes—can also create this vibrational experience.

Rubbing a mallet over a crystal singing bowl is akin to rubbing your finger over the rim of a wine glass to create a ringing sound. Imagine a bowl ten times the thickness of a wineglass and made up of crushed quartz instead of crystal or glass. The bowl's shape and consistency allow the vibration to echo endlessly, creating the sound of a choir—hence the term "singing" bowl.

Most crystal singing bowls are made of quartz crystals with physical properties that cause them to amplify, conduct, and transform energy. This is why even today, quartz is used in computer chips, TVs, microphones, and watches. To craft a singing bowl, a master crystal-glassmaker shapes crushed quartz into a bowl whose size and design create the desired vibration—a particular musical note or notes, or a sound—that aligns with a specific energy center in the body.

The Healing Power of Sound

Whether metal or crystal, the bowls' vibrations resonate beyond the ear's ability to receive sound. It is the whole body that resonates, not simply the eardrum. So when a pure vibration ripples through every cell in your body for a few seconds, then minutes, then longer, a natural state of cellular alignment occurs.

This sound experience is less a form of meditation and more like a healing aural massage that creates a trancelike state that temporarily disconnects you from your thoughts, any other sounds, and—to a certain extent—your own body. The vibrations can continue rippling through your body for days, and the nurturing power of sound healing on a physical and emotional level is profound.

I have found that listening to bowls is most powerful for me after I have performed some emotional clearing or emotional release work that leaves me in a tender and vulnerable state. Then to have those sweet, safe sound waves ripple through me, gently caressing my wounds, is one of the most healing experiences in life. The master Tibetan bowl player Damien Rose is a dear friend of mine. His CD *Liquid Bells Singing Bowls* is a powerful journey into silence through the transformative power of sound. Damien also performed live on my first guided meditation CD, *Fill What Is Empty; Empty What Is Full*, bringing tears to my eyes with his devotion to this sacred art. You can feel his heart going into each vibration on the tracks that feature his acoustic healing bowl sounds.

The Chopra Center's founders, Deepak Chopra and David Simon, developed a series of 12 signature Ayurvedic massage treatments, and one of them is a crystal singing bowl massage known as the *Gandharva*. In Hindu mythology, gandharvas were celestial musicians who performed exquisitely pleasing music for the gods at their palace banquets. They also acted as intermediaries, who flew through the sky, carrying messages between humans and the gods.

When I first came to the Chopra Center for the Journey into Healing workshop, I scheduled a massage for every day during the lunch break. On the first day, I selected the Gandharva. Oh my lord! First, my healing arts master blanketed me with warm, herbalized essential oil to balance me. Then after I had melted into the table, she opened my energy fields using various traditional Ayurvedic massage techniques, such as *abhyanga, vishesh, srota,* and *marma* therapy. At the same time, she intermittently played a crystal singing bowl, whose vibration permeated every cell in my being. It was unlike any other massage I have ever experienced, and I've been hooked ever since. When you are opened so completely and the bowl is playing, it is one of the most healing sensations you will ever experience.

The Gandharva is a deeply meditative experience and for hours after the treatment ends, the vibrations continuously return you to the present moment. Even days later, you continue to feel the vibrations ripple like waves lapping the shores of your bodymind. The impact of the vibrations on your bodymind is very real, and the effect they have on the brain simply through the healing power of sound is irrefutable. But unfortunately, unless you live with a healing arts master, this type of meditation massage therapy cannot realistically become part of your daily routine.

Yet sound is recognized as a powerful tool that can paradoxically take us deeper into stillness and silence. So that I can access the power of sound at a moment's notice, I recorded a loop of oms and bowls that I play if I'm having a particularly turbulent day. Closing my eyes and listening to this wave of all-consuming vibrations always brings stillness to my being and a smile to my face. Scientifically, the sound is vibrating through every aspect of your being, creating a sort of coherence as it vibrates equilibrium into each cell. At a certain point, the outside world is saying "Om," and so is your inner world. You can download it for free at **davidji.com**.

The Science of Sound Waves

Thousands of people use sound-wave recordings to meditate, and many have found this to be a very positive practice in their lives. Over the last 20 years, I have had many sound-wave meditation sessions that created deep states of relaxation for me and moved me into deep stillness. I have been part of several studies in which I was hooked up to biofeedback monitors that showed, as I listened to sound waves through headphones, my brain waves slowing, creating a deeper state of relaxation. In fact, modern science has confirmed that specific sound waves create specific brain-wave patterns. However, given the current limitations of scientific understanding, there is the obvious assumption but not yet *conclusive evidence* that particular brain-wave patterns indicate a specific state of consciousness.

Advocates of sound-wave meditation point to evidence that playing a vibration can create a certain brain wave pattern in your head, which then reflects a certain state of consciousness. Essentially, play the vibration, and the brain will respond accordingly and attune. And so it would logically follow that once you're attuned, you will experience the intended brain-wave state of consciousness of the wave being heard. For example, gamma waves have long been associated with states in which one takes things less personally, senses the dissolution of one's ego, or has an overwhelming feeling of universality or one-ness. So logic would conclude that by playing gamma waves, one would experience the characteristics of those universal states. There are several studies that either point to this correlation or imply it. Since science has not yet figured out how to determine the state of consciousness in someone else's brain or mind, there is currently only anecdotal evidence that this technique has scientific validity. Yet thousands use sound waves to meditate, and many have found this to be a very positive practice in their lives.

As I mentioned, I have been hooked up to biofeedback monitors to determine that my brain moved even deeper, reflecting theta waves, but again, determining that I achieved a specific state of consciousness is difficult. Here's essentially how it works.

BETA WAVES

In our normal waking state, our brain produces beta waves. In fact, we pretty much live our waking lives in beta state—a state of waking alertness characterized by busy or anxious thinking and active concentration. When the brain is in the beta state, also known as beta rhythm, its frequency can be recorded on a brain-wave monitor known as an electroencephalogram (EEG). The frequency range of beta waves is 13 to 30 cycles per second. You don't have to memorize that; it's purely for comparative purposes as we explore other brain-wave rhythms, and you can view the following chart, which shows all the waves and frequencies.

ALPHA WAVES

When we are relaxed, the rhythm of our brain waves slows down. As the activity slows to a frequency below 13 cycles per second, we enter a state known as alpha. This is defined as an intensely pleasurable and relaxed state of consciousness associated with deep physical and mental relaxation. On an EEG, the alpha state is defined by a pattern of smooth, regular electrical oscillations in the brain that occur when a person is awake and relaxed. In contrast to the more active frequency of beta waves on an EEG, alpha waves, also known as alpha rhythm, have a frequency range of 8 to 13 cycles per second.

During a sound-wave meditation, as we move from the beta brain-wave state of normal waking consciousness to the slower brain-wave pattern associated with our alpha state, one can sense a powerful shift to a more surrendering state of consciousness expressed through physical relaxation and emotional openness.

THETA WAVES

Once the alpha state is achieved, some people choose to stay there as an antidote to stress or a method to calm themselves when they are experiencing agitation. Others, having experienced the relaxation of the alpha state, choose to drift deeper still. In some of the more popular sound-wave meditation techniques, the premise is that we can drift even deeper into stillness by further slowing the sound waves, thereby inducing the brain to slow its activity and create theta waves. Theta waves, which are thought to move even more slowly than alpha waves, are produced in the frequency range of 4 to 8 cycles per second.

When the brain is in theta rhythm, the sense of openness we experience in alpha expands even further to a state of more holistic or universal awareness. In theta state, we experience a state of suspension. Like the gentle tides of the surf—moving in, hesitating for a moment, and then drifting out—we drift back and forth from activity hovering over the line into stillness. Of course, we can never be aware of that deep stillness until we drift back to the alpha state and then we have a comparison point. We've all experienced those surreal moments just before we've drifted into sleep that seem dreamlike even though we're not really sleeping. This state is known as theta rhythm, and the ability to hover there for a few moments is akin to consciousness surfing . . . riding the edge, hanging on the precipice between the uplift of the wave and the churn of surf only inches below . . . being in total stillness in the midst of activity and witnessing it.

DELTA WAVES

At the slowest end of the brain-wave spectrum are the delta waves (0 to 4 cycles per second), which we experience in deep sleep, also known as slow-wave sleep. At this low frequency, we can experience what is known as lucid dreaming, where we are the witness to our dreams, simultaneously experiencing ourselves as both the subject and the object of the dream. In fact, as our understanding of low-frequency brain waves has evolved, it has led to several theories about meditation and brain-energy consumption.

GAMMA WAVES

Gamma waves are a pattern of brain waves with a frequency range of 80 to 100 cycles per second. That's right: much higher than the beta waves of our waking state, which are a mere 13 to 30 cycles per second. According to current research, gamma waves appear to reflect the harmony or synchronization of various interconnected neural networks within you: essentially, your brain at peak performance. So even though the frequency range is at the high end of the sound-wave spectrum (five to seven times faster than beta waves), the brain is in an optimal receptive state to push the boundaries of awareness as it accesses information in new and different ways.

Although at opposite ends of the sound-wave activity spectrum, both delta (at the low end) and gamma (at the higher end) wavelengths have been thought to harmonize states of euphoria and of even deeper one-ness by briefly putting the brain into a state in which it is highly receptive and totally aware while it consumes power at an infinitesimally low rate. This has been referred to in the scientific community as the "zero power hypothesis," and this is what is happening when you drift into the gap in meditation. In short, it's a state in which you have disconnected from brain activity. In essence, you are using close to zero brainpower. Some researchers believe that in this state, you become less of your self and more of your *Self* as you move further from your personal brain activity and the concepts and perspectives of an individual, and closer to a more universal and expanded perspective.

Brain Waves and Their
Connection to States of Consciousness

While we cannot determine an individual's state of conscious-ness by simply observing them, scientific analysis tools such as EEGs can help us understand the presumed state of consciousness. The following chart illustrates the correlations.

Wave	Wave Frequency, cycles per second	Presumed State of Consciousness
Delta	0–4	Deep sleep/subtle witness to dreams
Theta	4–8	Universal or witnessing awareness
Alpha	8–13	Awake and relaxed
Beta	13–30	Active waking state
Gamma	80–100	Expanded/unity awareness/ universal cognition

A compelling study on the effects of long-term meditation on the brain was carried out at the University of Wisconsin by the neu-roscientist Richard Davidson. Published in 2004 in the *Proceedings of the National Academy of Sciences*, the study investigated the brain-wave patterns of eight Tibetan monks. The monks were hooked up to EEGs with more than 250 sensors, told to meditate on "uncondi-tional compassion" as the object of their attention, and then given MRI brain scans. The monks, who were handpicked by His Holiness the Dalai Lama, had undergone training in the Tibetan Nyingmapa and Kagyupa traditions of meditation and had spent an estimated 10,000 to 50,000 hours in meditation, over time periods ranging from 15 to 40 years. A control group of 10 student volunteers with no previous meditation experience were also tested after one week of training. Davidson and his researchers found that meditation activated the brain waves of the monks in significantly different ways than those of the volunteer students. During meditation, the monks produced much greater and more powerful gamma waves than the students, who showed only a slight increase in gamma-wave activity. But even the behavior of the waves was different, moving through the monks' brains in a more coordinated and organized pattern than in the students' brains. It's also important to note that the monks who had spent the most years meditating exhibited the highest levels of gamma waves. Equally significant is the fact that even when the monks were not meditating, the gamma signal in their brains stayed active. Their brains were different from those of the students, with stronger waves associated with problem solving, consciousness, and perception.

The Adaptable Brain

The Davidson study also demonstrated that the mental training and neural coordination a meditation practice (and presumably other disciplines) delivers can itself change the inner workings and circuitry of the brain in the area that is thought to control our focus, memory, learning patterns, and our perception of consciousness. Davidson's study clearly demonstrated a strong correlation between higher mental activity, a sense of heightened awareness, and gamma waves. While scientists used to believe that the brain was hardwired at a young age and couldn't create new neurons or new neural paths, an abundance of research that includes many studies on meditation has now proven that the brain is incredibly adaptable and dynamic and can change throughout one's life, a quality known as neuroplasticity.

Researchers at Harvard and Princeton have begun testing some of the monks who participated in Davidson's study, looking at different aspects of their meditation practice, including their ability to visualize images and control their thinking. And Davidson's vast research (which I elaborated on in Chapter 3) has sparked others to explore these concepts, and over the next few years, I expect that hundreds of other studies will provide further evidence of neuroplasticity.

While many advocates of sound-wave meditation say that lis-tening to a specific vibration creates certain brain-wave patterns that reflect a certain state of consciousness, it is, in fact, currently impossible to determine the state of consciousness in someone else's mind or brain. That could change next week; but for now, it's all up to interpretation.

Sound-Wave Audio Technology

There are many pioneering sound-wave technology companies that have introduced lower or deeper carrier frequencies such as delta waves and high-quality gamma-wave audio recordings to induce meditation. One of the most well-known companies in the realm of sound-wave meditation is the Counterpointe Research Institute, which produces the popular audio meditation program known as the Holosync Solution™. Many of my students began with Holosync or one of the other sound-wave meditation tech-nologies and then moved on to a mantra practice, ultimately feel-ing they were ready for a more personal, no-gear-required method to go within. But they took their first step into meditation because listening to sound waves seemed like an easy method.

I have experimented at length with many wave frequencies to move me from one brain-wave state to another. I have expe-rienced many deep sessions where theta and delta waves were played through headphones or speakers for hours on end. In 2005, David Simon and I experimented at length with theta-, delta-, and gamma-wave recordings and experienced very deep relaxation, intense meditations, and some powerful releases. However, I never experienced the depths of stillness and silence that I now experi-ence in my "no equipment necessary" meditation practice, where I truly surrender to my own stillness and silence.

For many of my students who began meditating using sound, they now prefer a daily practice that they can do without addi-tional equipment, and one that offers them opportunities to drift into unity consciousness on their own, whether they are high on a mountaintop, by the ocean, or at a friend's house. But for those who want to have meditation done "to" them, or who are looking to take a first step, sound-wave practices can open your eyes to the possibilities and, in the process, offer some very cool experiences.

Sound meditations can help you surrender.

CHAPTER SEVEN

SECRETS OF ENERGY MEDITATION

---

*"You have become so overflowing with love,
with compassion, and you want to share.
It happens at the fourth center, the heart.
That's why even in the ordinary world people
think love comes out of the heart. For them it
is just hearsay, they have heard it; they don't know
it because they have never reached to their heart.
But the meditator finally reaches to the heart."*

— OSHO

Throughout time, many have meditated using their connection to the energy centers in and outside of the body. There are hundreds, if not thousands, of ways to awaken, harness, release, and connect to your own energy through meditation. The most popular and most pervasive is the chakra meditation known as chakra tuning or chakra toning. I took my first step into that realm more than a decade ago, when I stumbled into what I thought was a simple hatha yoga class that turned out to be a two-hour chakra awakening session. In that class, I learned that according to ancient Vedic wisdom, there are seven major energy centers in the body. These are known as chakras, a term that derives from the Sanskrit word *cakram,* meaning "turning" or "wheel."

What Are Chakras?

The traditional Indian healing system known as Ayurveda teaches that the chakras are the energetic junction points connecting our local domain world of form and phenomena with the nonlocal realm of the unmanifest. The ancient Vedic texts of the later Upanishads, a core philosophical scripture of Hinduism, state that there are 108 chakras in and outside of the body. There are seven main chakras within the body that are said to be the energy centers. They radiate like wheels of light outward from a point on the physical body and through the layers of the subtle body (mind) and causal body (spirit) in an ever-increasing, fan-shaped or heart-shaped formation. These points are thought to be the focal points for the reception and transmission of our vital life force energy, known as *prana* in Sanskrit.

The seven main chakras are aligned in a column that begins at the base of your spine and extends to the top of your head. They're located symmetrically up your body, each of them spaced a distance of approximately seven fingers from each other, which is one hand and then two additional fingers from the tailbone to a bit below the navel, to the center of your chest (called the solar plexus), to your heart, to your throat, to the third eye (an inch or so above your eyebrows), and then to the crown of your head.

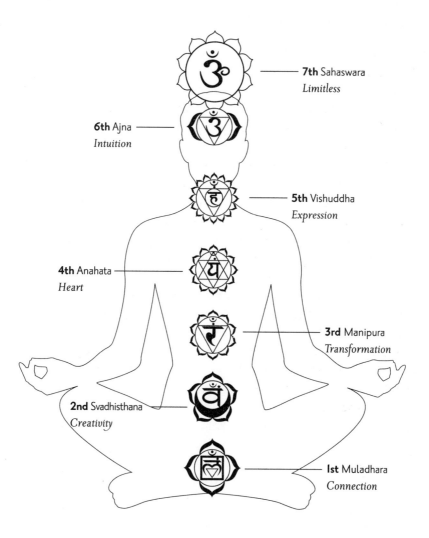

7th Sahaswara
Limitless

6th Ajna
Intuition

5th Vishuddha
Expression

4th Anahata
Heart

3rd Manipura
Transformation

2nd Svadhisthana
Creativity

1st Muladhara
Connection

In addition to the Vedas, other wisdom traditions from Asia, the Middle East, and even North America have integrated the chakras into their cultures. For example, the heart-expanding philosophy of Sufism rooted in ancient Turkey and Persia refers to four of these chakras as having powerful personalities. Accordingly, in these traditions, the navel chakra is called the "Self"; the heart chakra is "secret"; the throat chakra is "mysterious"; and the crown chakra is "the Teacher." The Hopi Indians of North America also speak of these same four chakras and describe them as being located on the crown of the head and in the regions of the throat, heart, and navel.

The Colors and Vibrations of Chakras

Each chakra has a specific color associated with it, as well as a vibrational mantra that opens or tunes the energy flow in each of our energy centers. This tuning is similar to opening up additional lanes on a highway. When the traffic has broader bandwidth, it can flow more easily and quickly. Master chakra scholars such as Anodea Judith and Karla Refoxo have explored the origins of the ancient chakra practice and have eloquently explained the deeper meanings, expanded characteristics, and personal affirmations of each chakra. Anodea has created DVDs, books, and even workshops on the subject. Karla has lived in the holy enclave of Nepal, crafting spiritually charged chakra amulets to connect people more deeply to their most divine selves.

Chakra meditation is extremely powerful, because it opens you up to a more universal flow at the level of your personal physiology, your emotional state, and your spiritual awareness. Let's explore each of the seven main chakras in a little more detail to set the foundation for the meditation. In the Vedic tradition, they start with the most earthbound and weighty and move upward to the more subtle, getting lighter and lighter until they reach the state of pure ether.

FIRST CHAKRA

The first chakra, also called the root or base chakra, is known in Sanskrit as the *muladhara* (pronounced "moola-dara"). This is your personal connection to groundedness, stability, and connection, and it is the heaviest of chakras. It is located at the tip of the tailbone and is essentially your contact point to the earth when you sit on the floor or ground. This is the site of your physical connection to the world. Traditionally, the muladhara is associated with the color red. During a chakra tuning, this root is where the foundational flow of all of the universe's energy enters you. So the flow of anything from the unmanifest, the unseen, the unbirthed, or the infinite enters here. The vibration or mantra for the first chakra is Laam.

Second Chakra

The second chakra, also called the sacral or sex chakra, is known in Sanskrit as the *svadhisthana* (pronounced "svah-dee-shtana") chakra. This is your personal connection to creativity—your own and that of the universe. It is located three fingers below your navel. Traditionally it is associated with the color orange. The most powerful energy on the planet is creative energy. It is the energy of birth that transforms the unmanifest into the manifest, thought into action, concept into product, idea into utterance, and desire into fulfillment.

When the second chakra is balanced, you are full, abundant, and pregnant with possibilities. You move in the direction of your dreams, and you know that you are deserving of them. The vibration or mantra for the second chakra is Vaam.

Third Chakra

The third chakra, also called the solar plexus chakra, is known in Sanskrit as the *manipura* (pronounced "monny-poora"). This is your "moving forward and following through" chakra that takes you in the direction of the seeds you've planted in the fertile ground of your second chakra. The manipura is located in the center of your chest at your solar plexus, a few inches below the joining of your ribcage. This is essentially the center of your body, where your emotional and physical digestive fires burn most brightly. This radiating power plant moves you toward your target and awakens your personal, internal strength to achieve your intentions and desires. Traditionally it is associated with the color yellow. This chakra has also been referred to as the sun or *surya chakra* (*surya* means "sun" in Sanskrit), because the golden yellow sun that radiates from the solar plexus is ever evolving, metabolizing, and transforming us in every moment.

When we harness the energy of the solar plexus chakra, we find empowerment and transformation. The vibration or mantra for the third chakra is Raam.

FOURTH CHAKRA

The fourth chakra, also called the heart chakra, is known in Sanskrit as the *anahata* (pronounced "anna-hatta") chakra. This is your personal connection to love (self-love and love for others), compassion, empathy, forgiveness, and peace. It is located in the area of your physical heart, a bit to the right of your left breast. You can place your hands on your heart right now and breathe in and feel the love you can shower the world with. That's your anahata—your true Buddha nature. Traditionally, it is associated with the color green.

The world could always use a bit more love; just like *we* could always use a bit more love. We never can have enough. If we feel we're being smothered by someone, most likely it is our resistance to his or her love that is constricting us and not the person's love itself. If we could open our hearts even a little each day, we would be happier, and those around us would feel that shift and share that energy. You actually can make a difference in the world each day by simply loving a bit more than you do right now. When we tap into our heart chakra, love radiates around us and out into the world.

Of course, to get the love flowing, you need to love yourself first, which is challenging for many of us. What's the challenge? We have built many barriers to receiving love. We tell ourselves, "I'm not worthy," "I don't deserve it," or, "Others deserve it more than me." Or sometimes we simply feel "less than."

If we are going to continue to share our gifts with the world, we need to fill ourselves first, so there's plenty of love to go around. It's similar to when you board a plane and the flight attendant says something along the lines of, "If the cabin decompresses, oxygen masks will drop down. If you're traveling with a child, please make sure you put the mask on yourself first before you place it on the child." This basic tenet of Buddhism, and apparently of most airlines, essentially says, "Fill yourself first, so you can serve the world. Be the river; be full; be abundant; fill yourself with love so it will overflow to others." Take a few minutes right now and practice the heart sutra meditation on page 103. You will absolutely feel a shift.

The vibration or mantra for the fourth chakra is Yaam. David Simon and several other Sanskrit scholars have also said the vibration can be pronounced as Yum.

Fifth Chakra

The fifth chakra, also called the throat chakra, is known in Sanskrit as the *vishuddha* (pronounced "vi-*shoo*-da") chakra. This is your personal connection to expression, expressing both your personal Self and your most universal Self. It is located at the center of your neck in the middle of your throat. Traditionally it is associated with the color blue.

The throat chakra is where we communicate, emote, and give ourselves permission to express. Congestion in the throat chakra is often a sign that you are repressing some aspect of yourself, not willing to admit something to yourself, or that you are withholding permission from yourself to do something. This is the chakra that is the last doorway to the lighter, higher chakras and the more ethereal nature of self. Before there can be a growth breakthrough or a step into the next chapter of your life, you must give yourself permission to move forward in some way—something you have long denied or repressed.

When this chakra opens, you have truly given yourself permission to let the universe work through you. The vibration or mantra for the fifth chakra is Haam. David Simon and Asian studies profes-sor and Vedic Master Yogi Claire Diab also pronounce this mantra as Hum. Either is considered correct.

SIXTH CHAKRA

The sixth chakra, also called the third-eye chakra, is known in Sanskrit as the *ajna* (pronounced *"ahjj-*na") chakra. This is your personal connection to source, to insight, intuition, essentially the doorway to what the ninth-century sage Adi Shankara referred to as the "causal realm." It is located in the middle of the lower forehead, between your eyes and up a bit.

Traditionally, the sixth chakra is associated with the color purple. Throughout time, in many different cultures, there has been a distinct relationship between the third eye and mystical or spiritual properties. It is considered the connecting point between your personal soul and the universal spirit—essentially where all your discernment and intuition rests. The vibration or mantra for the sixth chakra is Shaam.

In her classic *Babel*, Patti Smith, the singer, songwriter, laureate, spiritual warrior, and rock and roll goddess, so eloquently described the magic of the third eye in this excerpt from her poem about the most famous ninja to ever have lived—Sandayu the Separate:

> Sandayu enters. He bends down and carves an eye in the smooth forehead of his smiling wife. Hand in hand they walk through the garden. Then she blinks, then focuses on the face of her husband, sweet light of nostrils, he is seen at last! Thus found he laughs and shakes the sky. He is no longer Sandayu the Separate but Momochi, carver of the third new eye.

SEVENTH CHAKRA

The seventh chakra, or crown chakra, is known in San-skrit as the *sahaswara* (pronounced "sah-ha-*swa*-rah") or thousand-petaled-lotus chakra. This is your connection to the unbounded, infinite, expanding flow of the universe. It is located at the crown of your head and is often depicted in art as the Hindu deity Shiva, spouting the Ganges River from the top of his head. Traditionally, it is associated with the color white or ultraviolet.

This is the chakra in which everything that has just flowed through you flows back out into the universe. When you have limiting beliefs, opening up the crown chakra allows you access to the entire universe of possibilities. This is you in your most universal state, surrendering your individuality and ego for cosmic consciousness and moving from multiplicity into one-ness. The vibration or mantra for the seventh chakra is Om.

There are some schools of chakra practice that use the vibration Om for the sixth chakra and teach that the vibration of the seventh chakra is beyond sound. Please feel free to follow the practice that feels most comfortable to you.

Chakra Tuning

To activate, open, release, or expand your chakras, you "tune" them by bringing your awareness to them, envisioning the color of the chakra, connecting to its particular intention, and then repeating the vibration or mantra associated with the chakra. I'm most familiar with the practice of starting from the root and working your way up through the chakras. In other traditions, such as Reiki energetic healing, practitioners are known to perform their tuning starting at the crown chakra and moving downward.

Lightness and Then Integration

The process of chakra practice is to move from the root to the crown—the most dense to the most subtle manifestations of your being—opening your energy pathways first in your heaviest, most physical, and most deeply grounded aspects of your existence and then moving upward to ever-lighter expressions of your being. In many practices, you then weave your way back down from the crown to the root to integrate the lightest parts of you back into your more dense chakras. *Yogastha kuru karmani. Established in one-ness perform action.* This attunement will open all your energy centers as wide as possible and then flow this energy at every level back through your energetic essence. The result? An openness, coherence, and lightness of being that floats through your physical body, your emotional, psychological, intellectual beings, and your soul.

Over the years, I have recorded many chakra meditations, and several can be found online. On my first CD of guided meditations, I created a healing chakra meditation called "Heal Your Body" that uses the chakra mantras and additional vibrations to take you to a deep place of physical and emotional healing. On my CD *Guided Affirmations: Channeling the Universe Through Your Chakras,* I was inspired by the artisanship of Karla Refoxo's Tulku Chakra Amulet Collection and the affirmations she has woven into the charged chakra amulets she creates in Nepal.

In those 70 minutes of "meditation," you open each chakra, and as you tune each one through the power of affirmations, you access the universal traits in each energy center to empower yourself. That chakra meditation is downloadable exclusively at **davidji .com** and **tulkujewels.com.**

There are many other CDs and DVDs that can offer you a chakra meditation that lasts from five minutes to an hour. Deepak Chopra created a beautiful CD set called *Chakra Balancing: Body, Mind, and Soul,* produced by the brilliant musician and didgeridoo master Adam Plack. The tracks are available through Donna D'Cruz's music production company, raSā music, known for its authentic, atmospheric quality, beautiful design, and elegant engineering. Whatever CD or download you choose, I encourage you to explore some form of chakra practice to experience a unique and healing opening.

Sutra Meditation

Sutras are mantras with meaning and are often comprised of multiple words. *Sutra* is the Sanskrit word for "stitch" or "suture" and is similar to a stitch binding two pieces of skin or cloth. In the realm of meditation, sutras connect your world of space and time to the world beyond space and time . . . from your physical realm to the ethereal, astral realm . . . from the local domain to the nonlocal domain . . . from the manifest realm to the unmanifest. Back and forth and back again.

The most effective sutra practice is one you do after meditation, when you are as still and silent as possible. Then you silently repeat the sutra as you move your awareness from one chakra to the next. Deepak Chopra taught me, as he has taught thousands of meditators around the world, to "drop the sutras" like dropping a pebble into a still pond and then letting the ripples radiate outward.

This dropping of the sutras is akin to flowing on an energy highway, where the chakras are the tollgates that you gently open with your present-moment awareness. At each junction, you subtly repeat the sutras as they weave themselves between the local and nonlocal realms. Then you move your awareness to the next chakra and drop another set of sutras, let them resonate for a few minutes, and move to the next chakra and drop another set of sutras there. You continue until you have done this for all seven chakras. This powerful ritual of first going into silence for 30 minutes creates the perfect pathway through which your energy effortlessly flows within you and without you as you sit in stillness.

THE HEART SUTRA MEDITATION

The Seduction of Spirit sutras are kept silent and are shared only through the oral, in-person tradition of teacher to student, so I will not share them here. But I am able to reveal the four sutras for the heart chakra, as Deepak has encouraged sharing these throughout the world for decades. They are *peace, harmony, laughter,* and *love.* During the heart chakra part of the sutra meditation, we gently drift our awareness to our heart, envision a green color, and silently repeat—or "drop"—each set of sutras four times.

There are four sutras for each chakra, and each rippling takes about 15 seconds. For example: peace (15 seconds), harmony (15 seconds), laughter (15 seconds), love (15 seconds). Rather than count between sutras, envision dropping the sutra into your heart as if it were a still pond. Then let the sutra slowly ripple until it stops (about 15 seconds). Then drop the next sutra, and let that ripple until you have dropped *peace, harmony, laughter,* and *love* four times. The slow rippling acts as a timer, readying you for dropping the next sutra. Doing the complete set of four sutras four times takes about four minutes.

Let's try it now. Bring your awareness to your heart. Envision a green color in that area. And now, very slowly, silently repeat with your eyes closed: peace, harmony, laughter, love; peace, harmony, laughter, love; peace, harmony, laughter, love; peace, harmony, laughter, love. Then just sit for a few moments, and let that settle in. When you notice that you've drifted away to thoughts, sounds, or physical sensations, very gently drift back to peace, harmony, laughter, and love. Let's meditate together.

How does that feel? Do you feel any different? If you can tack this ritual onto the end of your morning meditation, within days your heart will begin to open a little bit more. You will feel a greater sense of compassion, be more forgiving, and flow with a lighter sense of being. And you will actually experience greater peace, harmony, laughter, and love.

There are seven chakras and seven corresponding sets of sutras. So even if you've never attended the Seduction of Spirit meditation retreat, you can perform the heart sutras (see the previous sidebar) as part of your daily practice, and your life will begin to become happier and more loving. What you think, you become. And the heart sutras are powerful affirmations to evolving you to a life of greater love and compassion. Simply go into meditation, and after you have been in stillness and silence for 30 minutes, stop repeating your mantra or following your breath. Just float for a bit. And when your heart and soul are as defenseless and vulnerable as they can be, surrender to silently repeating peace, harmony, laughter, and love. Gently drop each sutra like dropping a pebble into a still pond. Peace . . . harmony . . . laughter . . . love. And do that four times.

Deepak taught me to do this with a different set of sutras for each chakra, meditating for a total of 58 minutes (30 minutes of mantra meditation; 28 minutes of sutras) every morning and afternoon for a week. After seven days of this meditation immersion, you will be able to calmly meditate in the middle of New York City's Times Square! Ten years later, I am still practicing them and virtually everything I desire unfolds effortlessly in my life.

The effectiveness of the sutras is most powerfully activated when they are dropped into stillness and silence. That is the most fertile soil for intentions to sprout in. For the full impact of the sutras, I recommend that you append this heart sutra practice to the end of your daily meditation practice. Do this for a week, and your life will change. You'll never want to stop.

Let's get a sampling by performing a chakra tuning right now. For this meditation, feel free to sit comfortably in a chair and read it to yourself or lie down and stream it directly from **davidji.com** on the section exclusively for readers of *Secrets of Meditation*.

Start by taking a few long, slow, deep breaths in and out. Once you feel you have settled down a bit, close your eyes for a moment, and envision the chakras in their special places within your body and glowing the color associated with each energy center. See all seven of them radiating: the root . . . red; the sacral chakra . . . orange; the solar plexus . . . yellow; the heart chakra . . . green; the throat chakra . . . blue; your third eye . . . purple; the crown chakra . . . ultraviolet . . . an opalescent white light. Now gently bring your awareness to the base or root chakra—in Sanskrit it's known as the muladhara chakra. Its color is red and the vibration is LAAM. As you envision the energetic flow and the color, say it with me slowly, and let the vibration last like chanting an Om.

Laam. Laam. Laam. Let's settle in for a few moments and just breathe.

We've just awakened our energy of connection, groundedness, and stability. This foundational energy must be strong to act as the platform for all energetic flow throughout the body. With each beat of your heart, feel the strong, red pulse of the muladhara, channeling the energy of wholeness, stability, and balance. See yourself as a conduit for the life force. You are a vessel for this flow of chi, qi, or prana. It journeys through your energy centers, strengthening with each pulse as it moves in you, throughout you, through you.

Next, bring your awareness from your tailbone to a place a few inches below your belly button. This is the second or sacral chakra; in Sanskrit, it's known as the svadhisthana chakra. This is your center of creativity, of birthing new healing aspects of your self. This is where your nourishing decisions come from. This is the font of all your creative energy.

Its color is orange, and with each breath, you can feel the orange expansion of your svadhisthana chakra. The vibration is Vaam. As you envision the energetic flow and the color, say it with me slowly. Vaam. Vaam. Vaam. Let's settle in for a few moments and just breathe. Radiating out and through each cell, this is the energy of awakening, birth, growth, expansion, and nourishment. This energy center acts as the fertile soil for the birth of infinite possibilities and the pure potentiality of creation from nothing.

Now bring your awareness to the solar plexus chakra—the center of your torso. In Sanskrit, it's known as the manipura chakra. Its color is yellow like the sun, and the vibration is Raam. As you envision the energetic flow and the color, say it with me slowly. Raam. Raam. Raam. Let's settle in for a few moments and just breathe. We've just awakened our energy of forward movement, of seeing things through, of getting it done. This is the Pitta chakra—the chakra of our inner fire, known in Sanskrit as *agni*. This metabolic energy must be strong to consume all emotional and physical ingestions, cook them, transform them, access what nourishes us, and let go of what no longer serves us. With each beat of your heart, feel the strong yellow fire of the manipura.

When the inner fire of manipura chakra is weak or blocked, we may feel tired, frustrated, and withdrawn. We're scared to take risks and confront people or issues. We don't have enough energy to plant and nourish the seeds of our intentions and desires, so they are unable to germinate and flourish.

By strengthening the power of our manipura chakra, we nourish the inner fire that burns away whatever is no longer serving us, including limiting beliefs, ideas, and memories. This will allow your life energy to flow freely so that you can experience the joyful energy that fuels all your intentions and helps you realize your deepest dreams and desires.

Now move your awareness from your solar plexus to your heart chakra. To find it, simply place your hand on your heart. That's where your loving energy radiates from. In Sanskrit, it's known as the anahata chakra. This is your center of compassion—your true Buddha nature. This is where your ability to *be* peace, *love* unconditionally, *trust* in the divine, and, most important, to *forgive* resides. This includes not just forgiving others but forgiving yourself as well.

Its color is green—and with each breath, feel a green pulse of pure love wash through your body. The vibration is Yaam. As you envision the energetic flow and the color, say it with me slowly. Yaam. Yaam. Yaam. Let's settle in for a few moments and just breathe.

Next, drift your awareness to the throat chakra, located in front of your neck. In Sanskrit, it's known as the vishuddha chakra, and it governs your expression and your ability to give yourself permission in all areas of your life. This chakra is associated with the dream state of consciousness. Its color is deep blue, and the vibration is Haam. As you envision the energetic flow and the color, say it with me slowly. Haam. Haam. Haam. Let's settle in for a few moments and just breathe. We've just awakened our energy of communication and expression. Constrictions in this area often prevent us from clearly expressing ourselves to others, and a total constriction indicates that you haven't given yourself permission to speak. The vishuddha must be strong so that all the energy created in the body has a place to express itself.

Next move your awareness from your throat to the place right between your eyebrows and one inch up. This is your third eye chakra or ajna. It sits in the middle of your forehead and connects you to your spiritual energy.

Its color is purple, and the vibration is Shaam. As you envision the energetic flow and the color, say it with me slowly. Shaam. Shaam. Shaam. Let's settle in for a few moments and just breathe. We've just awakened our energy that connects us to spirit. The ajna must be open and clear to see into the future and to allow us to trust the universe.

Now shift your awareness from your third eye to the crown of your head. This is known as your crown chakra or sahaswara—the thousand-petaled lotus. In this state, there is no activity of the mind—no knower, no knowledge, and nothing to be known. Knowledge, knower, and known all become unified and liberated.

Its color is pure ultraviolet light, and the vibration is Om. As you envision the energetic flow and the color, say it with me slowly. Om. Om. Om. Let's settle in for a few moments and just breathe. We've just awakened the energy that connects us to unboundedness, all-knowing, all-seeing, pure consciousness. The sahaswara chakra must be wide open to allow the energy from the tailbone to the crown to freely flow in, out, and through the body.

By chanting all of these vibrations, you have opened and aligned your energy centers. There still may be some congestion and some constriction, so perform this chakra tuning with regularity and your healing will accelerate. Right now, let's activate our body's own natural healing properties by feeling the sacred energy flow through from the root to the second chakra to the solar plexus to the heart to the throat to the third eye to the crown. When the constrictions have been opened, the energy effortlessly flows through you on a journey of reawakening your wholeness.

Just sit and take a few moments to witness your bodymind. Notice what you feel and how you interpret it. You may want to journal or simply let the awakened energy flow continue to reverberate. Whatever you choose to do, always be gentle with yourself after you've meditated or performed a chakra tuning. With your eyes open or closed, just sit for a few moments, and let the stillness and silence settle in. Don't leap up to answer the phone, and don't feel the need to end the meditation until you are ready. And for energy meditations or chakra tunings, listen to your bodymind, and don't drive or operate heavy machinery immediately following the practice.

You can perform chakra tuning anytime by closing your eyes, putting your attention on each chakra, and bringing an intention to it. This can be in the form of chanting, speaking, whispering, or silently repeating an affirmation (*I am creative, I am worthy of love, I am whole*, and so on), a mantra (*om mani padme hum, aham brahmasmi, so hum,* and so forth), sutras (*peace, harmony, laughter, love*), or the sounds of each chakra (*Laam, Vaam, Raam,* and so forth). Just the simple act of combining (1) single-pointed attention on your chakras and (2) the subtle intention to open and receive will bring an expansion into your energetic relationship with the world.

Energy meditations can help you awaken and open.

CHAPTER EIGHT

SECRETS OF SENSORY MEDITATION

"We should be blessed if we lived in the present always, and took advantage of every accident that befell us, like the grass which confesses the influence of the slightest dew that falls on it; and did not spend our time in atoning for the neglect of past opportunities, which we call doing our duty. We loiter in winter while it is already spring."

— HENRY DAVID THOREAU

Sensory meditation focuses on taking in the world around you through your body and celebrates being present to a particular sensory experience. Sensory meditation uses one or several of the five senses—listening to sounds, soft gazing, inhaling aromas, feeling with your hands or other body parts, and tasting—to fully experience the present moment. By allowing the sensations of a particular sensory organ to become the object of attention, the messages transmitted by our other sensory organs just drift away. The sense becomes an overt conduit for all information coming into your body, and all of your thoughts melt into the precious present moment as it unfolds.

Through this practice, you can learn how to develop a deeper awareness using your senses. In time, this awareness will offer you insights into an aspect of yourself that rests beneath your senses—your energetic self—known in Sanskrit as the *pranamaya kosha*. Literally, *prana* means vital energy; *maya* means illusion; and *kosha* means layer. So this aspect of yourself is the illusionary layer of vital energy!

We've already explored the secrets of sound and sight meditation in a specific practice, yet we have the ability in every moment to simply witness through our ears and eyes and experience the same object from different perspectives . . . to see our world with new landscapes . . . with new eyes and ears! Take a few moments for the next few days and stop . . . look around . . . fix your gaze on something either very familiar or something totally unfamiliar . . . and stay with it for several minutes. Keep using it as a drishti, and immerse into its being with a soft gaze and then merge yourself into its shape, texture, pattern, structure, color, thickness, density, relationship to things next to it, and its essence. Additionally, over the next several days, do this with sounds you hear. You can use only sounds of nature—birdcalls, boots in snow, rustling of leaves in the wind, rain falling, dog barking, the splashing of ocean waves. Or allow any sound to become the object of your attention, including train whistles, car horns, leaf blowers, plane engines, and highway traffic. They are all simply vibrations.

"Clarity. Clarity of vision. What you've been looking at from the wrong angle and not seeing at all."

— THE EDGE, U2

Aroma and tasting meditations are more like experiential immersions rather than meditations, but they can be a sweet doorway to present-moment awareness. In aroma meditations, the object of your attention is your nose and the gentle breath that wafts into your nostrils. This inhalant can be anything: the earthy aromas of a pine- or cedar-filled forest; the intense, snaking smoke ribbon of incense; the subtle, intoxicating fragrance of essential oils; the salty mist of the ocean frothing at the shore; the aromatic bouquet that lifts from a curry sizzling in a a copper karahi; even the comforting first whiffs of our morning coffee brewing.

Secrets of Aroma Meditation

Our connection to smells and the meaning they have carved into our nervous system are profound. Olfaction is our most primal sense and in a nanosecond can trigger memories of our grandmother's freshly baked cookies, our grade-school teacher's perfume, or the musty cabin of our childhood summer camp. Events from decades ago are resurrected in our mind when the right aroma wafts into our nostrils. And we can also use distinct aromas to fully enter the present moment for short periods of time.

In an aroma meditation, you can choose to immerse yourself in one scent or in a series of different ones so you can better experience the depth of a particular smell by comparing it to another. This process awakens aspects of your nasal receptors that you may not have felt before. And it will consistently provide you with short bursts of present-moment awareness, though rarely one-ness.

The nose is so delicate that after extended periods of aroma immersion, our sensors become saturated, and we start to hit a sensory threshold. The complexity of that first inhalation becomes more subtle, and the intensity can only be recaptured after stepping away from the aroma for a while and letting our smelling ability "recharge." Another way to do this is to experience a flow of multiple smells, such as diverse and aromatic spices, herbs, or oils. But even with changing aromas, very quickly you hit the saturation point, and one smell bleeds into another.

At my first Ayurvedic cooking class, our chef cooked us through a guided meditation of all the spices used in his *masala,* a word that means "mixture" in Hindi, Urdu, and Bengali. Six of us sat in front of his cooking island, and he poured the raw ingredients one by one into our palms as we inhaled with our eyes closed. Then he poured the same ingredient into a sauté pan over a high flame and toasted it so the nutty, sharper quality of the spice filled the air around us. Next, he added a splash of oil to his pan, and the aroma changed one more time, becoming sweeter, richer, and in some cases, cloying. He proceeded to guide us in this awakening-the-senses meditation with a magnificent spice parade of white peppercorns, cloves, malabar leaves, pippali (long pepper), black cumin (known as *shahi jeera*), cumin seeds, cinnamon, green cardamom, nutmeg, star anise, and coriander seeds. With our eyes closed, we simply breathed first the raw, then the toasted, and then the sautéed spice. We sat and breathed with big smiles on our faces as the atmospheric quality of the room and our consciousness transformed with each spice, generating a new wave of aromatic awareness.

Secrets of Tasting Meditations

After we had been thoroughly enticed with the aromas of the spices, we dined on one of the most delicious meals I have ever tasted. The depth of flavor in each bite carried with it the subtlety of each phase of the spice's evolution within the cooking process. In its final form as a masala, each spice had its own flavor as well as its interplay with each of the other spices—as well as the merged flavor! With each bite . . . with each inhalation . . . I was so absorbed into the moment that time stood still. Every time I dine on Indian food (which sometimes is weekly), I experience a precious waft of that present-moment awareness infused with an aroma that carries with it the laughter and bliss of that meditation. Our senses of taste and smell are so primal, they can instantly transport us back to the moment and we will experience the same physiological sensations and emotions that we did the very first time. Whenever I smell any of those raw spices, I smile and feel comforted.

And, you can eat mindfully pretty easily no matter what you eat or where. Try it at an upcoming meal—truly savoring each bite, each chew, and each swallow. I encourage you to eat one meal a week in silence with no TV, no talking, no music, no reading material . . . just you and the food before you.

The challenge of quickly overloading a sense organ is also true for tasting food, and that is why champagne meditations and chocolate meditations have become so popular—you have to take baby steps, slowly savoring each inhalation, taste, sip, chew, lick, and swallow while staying totally mindful in the process. Living the sizzly tickle of a bubbly drop sliding down your throat, or feeling a chocolate truffle collapse on your tongue as the masala of earthy flavors melts into your being, the taste, the aroma, and the ritual all act as the object of your attention. In a chocolate-tasting meditation, you can delicately savor a truffle or another fine piece of chocolate as if it were the last piece of chocolate on earth, truly taking your time to feel its textures, density, aromas, complexity of flavors, and intricacy of fragrances until you are the chocolate . . . and it is you. You can perform this meditation alone or with others. I like to celebrate/meditate in this way at one meal a week at least.

What I've observed in all the food and aroma meditations that I have participated in is that our olfactory and gustatory systems are so primal that the process of identifying sensations and decoding them instantly pulses us back through all the tastes and smells of our past . . . not to this moment but from the actual moment to the memories we have of that sensory experience. So there is an aha! moment—that very first moment when the sumptuousness of the flavor explodes on your tongue or as the aroma first hits the back of your nose—but this is rarely a sustained period of present-moment awareness.

But even if these immersions don't provide the longer-lasting benefits of a non-sensory meditation practice, they still offer value: a fun way to be present. As long as you consciously stay mindful during these types of experiences—eating and drinking mindfully—they will nourish you and reinforce your ability to more consciously witness yourself and witness life. When we are able to more consistently witness our behaviors, we can see our non-nourishing behaviors in a more objective light, and rather than being defensive, we can then make more conscious, life-affirming choices.

Body Meditations

Mindfulness meditation, which we previously discussed, is a "body" meditation, because you are taking in energy and information from all of your senses—your hearing, seeing, smelling, tasting, breathing, and feeling everything in your body that you can feel, including the largest organ in your body: your skin. But there are also more intimate physical forms of meditation that involve the connection between two people, such as in partner yoga, massage, and lovemaking.

A truly gifted massage therapist can open up, step out of the way, and channel the universe in a dynamic exchange of energy between themselves and the object of their attention. Giving someone a massage can be a meditation in itself. And surrendering to the nurturing and healing touch of massage treatment is certainly one of the most stress-relieving things you can do as you open your physiology and your heart a bit. Receiving a massage is a fully present-moment-awareness experience. Regardless of where your mind wanders, you are continuously brought back to the object of your attention: wherever you are being touched in a given moment and whatever energetic or emotional connection the sensation of touch triggers.

There are thousands of books and videos on massage, so I will defer to these experts on "the best" or "the most effective" modalities of massage. Over the last decade, I have become most familiar with traditional Ayurvedic massage, which uses warm, herb-infused oil designed to balance one's mind-body personality. The healing arts masters trained at the Chopra Center for Wellbeing have all learned to perform sacred Ayurvedic bodymind meditation therapies, not to simply give massages. It is a wonder to behold: they truly believe they are in the presence of the body of the divine spirit when they are providing massage therapies. To be on the receiving end of their meditation is a meditation in itself. I've spent substantial amounts of time traveling in the Far East and receiving many types of massage throughout the Philippines, Thailand, Vietnam, Cambodia, and India, yet none compare.

I'm honored to have been on the receiving end of hundreds of these treatments from these truly divine Ayurvedic healing masters: Maureen Sutton, Grace Wilson, Kelly Luvera, Angela Smith, Bess O'Conner, Bridget McKenna, April Stickelman, Misty Murray, Jillian, Nicole King, Josie, Kathryn, Nicole Gabrielle, Jenny Lisa,

Merwan Ramsden, Kelie Micho, and my dear friend and brilliant bodymind/energy worker Jennifer Johnson—all at the Chopra Center in California; Kate and Rene from the Chopra Center in New York; and Melissa from the spa at the Grove Park Inn in Asheville, North Carolina. Over the years, these therapists have used their most healing energy and nurturing touch to subtly open my physical body, my mind, and my soul and then brilliantly guide me to surrender into one-ness. They have done this for countless others from all over the world. Many of them have left the spas they worked at to share their gifts with new communities. Should you ever find yourself under the nurturing touch of any of these healers, consider yourself blessed, and prepare to be transported.

I am also a devotee of Thai massage, which is most often practiced clothed. It is similar to having someone do yoga to you. Your Thai massage therapist actually moves you into positions akin to yoga asanas and then holds you in those positions as you breathe into them . . . merge into them as your body becomes theirs. Slowly and effortlessly you stretch, millimeter by millimeter, further than you otherwise thought you could. Stretch your body . . . stretch your mind . . . stretch your heart. The process is extremely expansive. And it is very easy under these circumstances to surrender to the present moment.

Partner yoga has gained popularity over the years, birthing some very powerful offshoots such as family yoga and contact yoga. Contact Yoga, based on the healing power of love and intimacy, was founded by American yogini and philanthropist Tara Lynda Guber, who also created Yoga Ed., the nationally recognized yoga-for-schools program that forever changed ghetto schools into temples of mindfulness starting with South Central Los Angeles. (Imagine . . . metal detectors are removed from schools and replaced with shelving for yoga mats. That's transformation!) Contact Yoga acts as a powerful body meditation as you use partnering poses to explore *relationship* in your life . . . your deepest patterns of connecting and distancing, loving and protecting, giving and receiving—patterns that usually remain unconscious until they are brought into the light of yoga. Tara and co-author Anodea Judith have taken these teachings to the masses with their book *Contact: The Yoga of Relationships,* which brilliantly explores and explains the physical, emotional, and spiritual awakenings that can occur through the practice of the seven points of contact: trust, passion, commitment, love, communication, vision, and union. Practicing Contact Yoga can be a powerful personal development tool and a body-centered meditative experience.

The Yoga of Sex

For thousands of years, sex, the act of lovemaking, even the moment of orgasm have all been described as meditative experiences because of the wave of present-moment awareness that sweeps through the participants. Lovemaking can be a meditation if the shared focus is the journey and not the destination, moving from an expectation to the preciousness of each moment, where the object of your attention is each breath and every physical movement you experience. In that kind of atmosphere, the practice takes on a powerful body*mind* connection as our physical experience flows into an emotional experience. The moment of orgasm has been defined as pure, present-moment awareness, where your thoughts are not in the past or future but in the now!

Unfortunately, that present moment only lasts a few moments, but the actual act of lovemaking can last for hours, keeping the present moment alive as each lover moves through wave after wave of merging two physical bodies into one. The ancient Hindu treatise on sexual behaviors known as *The Kama Sutra* is considered the most well-known guide on love, lovemaking, and the sexual act. Sexual meditation is essentially a form of body-centered restful awareness that is a fusion of static and dynamic prana, or life force, within our bodies. Although nourishing chemicals and nurturing hormones are released into the bloodstream during this sensory voyage, it is one of activity—more so of mindfulness (paying attention to the activity all around and within) rather than of stillness.

Tantric Meditation

The wise sage Osho once said, "Yoga is suppression with awareness; tantra is indulgence with awareness." Tantra is a body of ritualized spiritual mysticism and esoteric study that has survived for millennia. Tantra is historically not a single coherent system but rather a school of thought—almost tribal in nature—within both Hinduism and Buddhism. Tantra deals primarily with spiritual practices and ritual forms of worship that aim at liberation from ignorance and *samsara* (the cycle of rebirth). Several obscure offshoots of Hindu tantra have embraced sensory celebration and sexual meditations as ways to expand, grow, and achieve higher states of consciousness. In fact, the Sanskrit word "tantra" comes from two Sanskrit words: *tanoti*—"stretch" or "expand," and *trayati*—"liberation."

The science of tantra has two main branches or paths: *vama marga* (the "left-hand way") and *dakshina marga* (the "right-hand way"). Vama marga, the left path, combines sexual life with yoga practices in order to connect the energy of the universe with the primal energy within us. Dakshina marga, the right path, is yoga without sexual connection. In several left-path Tantric sects, various sexual practices and rituals are described in detail as devotional offerings to the goddess Shakti. One ritual is participating in the sexual rites of vamamarga, a fusion of masculine and feminine energies leading to an ecstatic spiritual experience. The seamless fusion of opposing sacred energies (creating one-ness) is considered a path to enlightenment, and the nonphysical, spiritual orgasm that occurs is a glimpse of this higher state of consciousness . . . one of pure bliss—beyond ecstasy.

The sexual union practices of early Hindu tantra known in Sanskrit as *maithuna* (pronounced "my-t'huna") were designed for practitioners to evolve their personal sexual energy into sacred energy and to then achieve higher states of physical and spiritual awareness as they exchanged this sacred energy. As the two practitioners move deeper into maithuna, they reach ecstatic sexual states and lock into what is referred to as a static embrace. The orgasm in this ritual takes place when the transfer of spiritual energy between the two practitioners culminates in the union of their subtle bodies. There is no physical ejaculation but a merging into one-ness of the Shiva (masculine) and Shakti (feminine) energies between the two of them, resulting in a united energy field.

Long ago, many of these Tantric rituals shifted from sexual practices in the physical realm to a more metaphorical and metaphysical practice without actual sexual penetration. It should also be noted that sexual rites were historically practiced only by a minority of Tantric sects. Yet our culture has embraced tantra with the misconception that tantra is all about sex. Modern expressions of tantra celebrate cosmic consciousness through the pleasure of the senses. Several offshoots of modern Tantric philosophy also celebrate the physical and emotional interrelationship between the Shiva (masculine) and Shakti (feminine) energy within and between two people. A powerful form of tantric sexual meditation is about awakening the god or goddess within—your most divine sensual aspect—giving yourself to another person in a devotional way and really taking the time . . . until time stands still . . . to use your senses to exchange energy with one another, merging two beings into one while you are both totally present. Regardless of what you choose to share, Tantric meditations are all about giving to one another and making sure that your bodies, minds, and spirits are on the same path.

As two people begin the practice of a lovemaking meditation, they set the intention for the experience to be a sacred journey in which they witness their own feelings and emotions, those of their partner, and the union of the two. This intention of sacredness and an ongoing awareness of each other's breaths, the rise and fall of each other's bellies, moisture awakening on the skin, the sound and sensation of the rapid beating of each other's hearts, words spoken and unspoken, the most subtle of aromas, tastes, and healing touch will move the couple to a higher plane of individual, empathetic, and collective consciousness. The sense of spiritual one-ness that is experienced when two people merge intimately into each other is akin to any aha! moment one can have. Just touching this level of unity once will help a couple move their relationship to another plane of existence. If nothing else, as you explore your emotions, your senses, and your sense of self with your partner through Tantric meditation, you will understand yourself better, and that is the perfect starting point for a relationship with another being. This is a wonderful meditation to use to strengthen and enhance your relationship with yourself as well as with your partner.

How Does Yoga Relate to Meditation?

Yoga means union. Therefore, yoga is meditation. And meditation is yoga. Any practice that brings about a state of present-moment awareness or a stilling of the mind is a form of meditation: that moment during running or cycling or swimming or dancing or writing or having an orgasm, or making a big sale, or riding a roller coaster, or practicing the eight limbs of yoga. That moment when you are totally present . . . in which there is no past or future, in which time has no meaning, where there is no thought, when you are totally in the zone . . . that moment when you are in total sync with your body, your mind, the moment, the universe. There is only a state of pure present-moment awareness. It is this one-ness that is the true definition of yoga—pure being, pure unity.

Most people think of yoga in terms of a physical practice that occurs on a mat in which you move your body into postures or poses known in Sanskrit as "asana" (pronounced "AH-sah-nah"). Then, depending on your school of practice and your philosophical orientation, you "live" the pose and then flow to the next. Each school of yoga spends varying amounts of time in the pose and also focuses on a select few of the hundreds of asanas. In this context, yoga has the ability to harness that dynamic interplay between stillness and activity. You breathe into the pose . . . you become the pose . . . you let yourself *be*. Asana is a truly beautiful expression of consciousness in motion.

But then you get back into the physical world and change poses. And then you change poses again. Over time, virtually every student of yoga develops an evolved homeostasis in the body's internal rhythms leading to better flexibility, focus, and balance; increased physical and mental confidence; often greater patience; increased strength; and powerful easing of the symptoms of PMS and of pre-, peri-, menopause, and postmenopause. Research performed in 2010–2012 has shown a connection between daily yoga practice and pain relief in cancer patients, hinting at the validity of increased immune function through breathing and asana. The resources section of **davidji.com** is continuously updated with the most cutting-edge scientific studies and clinical trials on yoga and meditation, especially for the treatment of pain. I invite you to visit and check out the various studies (Google "yoga pain study" or "yoga cancer study," and *thousands* of links will appear in the search results).

But stillness and silence during the practice is intermittent. In fact, it is usually *not* where most teachers take you during yoga class. But there are great teachers that give you permission to explore your being. And there are talented and intuitive teachers who can guide you to powerful experiences that open you, center you, relax you, invigorate you, awaken you, soften you, and expand you; this is why yoga is referred to as a practice of body-centered restful awareness.

Any practice that nourishes you, evolves you, and adds value to your life is worth exploring. I have been a practitioner, student, and teacher of myriad yogic practices from the four main paths of yoga: *raja, bhakti, karma,* and *gyan* (also referred to as *jnan* or *jnana* and pronounced "ghee-ahn"). Over the last few decades, I've enjoyed the asana practices of Anusara and Kundalini yoga; the rigor and spirit-infusion of Jivamukti, created by the magnificent yoga masters David Life and Sharon Gannon; and most recently, the Seven Spiritual Laws of Yoga, in which I became certified in 2011 with 61 other sweet yogis. I honor any student of any age or philosophy who ventures into a studio. Whether it's Kundalini, Anusara, Ashtanga, Bikram, Jivamukti, Iyengar, Vini-Flow, Swaroopa, hot yoga, Joe's yoga, or your own living room DVD yoga, the key is engaging in the practice.

One of my favorite yoga studios for many years was Kundalini East in Manhattan (on Broadway, right across the street from ABC Carpet and Home, where Deepak's East Coast salon—Deepak Home Base—is located). It was at Kundalini East in 2001 that I first embraced the beautiful practice of Kundalini yoga and immersed myself in the powerful translations of the Sikh visionary and master yogi, Guru Bhajan. Every class ended with all of us sipping sweet chai tea and gazing into each other's eyes with grins of joy as we radiated the vibrations of the past hour. The daily practice transformed my body and mind over the years. And whether I was at Kundalini East; or Starseed Yoga in Montclair, New Jersey; or a David Life class at Jivamukti; or a John Friend Anusara workshop; or even at my own Seven Spiritual Laws of Yoga teacher training at Chopra Center University, it was usually only at the end of the yoga class, during savasana (corpse pose), that I was able to finally disconnect from my body and mind, drift into stillness, and fully integrate the teachings as I experienced one-ness.

Many schools of yoga seem to emphasize getting a physical work-out or achieving perfect poses, which build our strength, flexibility, and balance yet keep us more focused in the physical realm. The Seven Spiritual Laws of Yoga—a spiritual, hatha yoga practice developed by Deepak Chopra, David Simon, and yogi Claire Diab—places greater emphasis on going deep into one's soul while in a particular pose, rather than achieving perfection in the asana. Throughout a Seven Spiritual Laws of Yoga class, we shift our awareness back and forth between silent stillness and dynamic physical activity.

Many styles of yoga, including the Seven Spiritual Laws of Yoga, incorporate a series of flowing asanas known as sun salutations, or *surya namaskar* in Sanskrit. But even during sun salutations, our moments of restful awareness are consistently brought back into the physical realm; it's distinctly the present moment, but alas, we are in the realm of activity . . . of unrest. Throughout any yoga practice, we return to the physical realm. And the fact that the practice is *body centered* keeps the practice in the physical realm. When we think of yoga we envision someone practicing an asana. But the practice of asana is only one aspect of yoga, which is a broad philosophy that encompasses all aspects of life. In the raja (royal) yoga tradition that developed in ancient India, the great yogic teacher, sage, and wisdom translator Patanjali defined yoga as *the cessation of all mental fluctuations; all wandering thoughts cease and the mind is focused on a single thought.*

Yoga's Eight Limbs

It was more than 2,000 years ago—sometime between 200 years before or after the death of Jesus Christ—that the foundations of yoga philosophy were written down by Patanjali in *The Yoga Sutras*. This sacred text describes an eight-limbed path that forms the structural framework for a program of right living. None of the eight limbs is more important than another, each being a part of a holistic regimen that brings a person into total wholeness of body, mind, and soul.

According to Patanjali, the postures or poses known as *asana* are just one of eight limbs of the practice of yoga, but there are seven others that are as important. The eight limbs (known in Sanskrit as *ashtanga*) are as follows:

1. *Yama:* Enlightened Conduct (Behavior)

The yamas are a universal code of commandments or moral imperatives (essentially the DO-NOTs) that describe evolutionary behavior or how enlightened beings should live their lives. In Sanskrit yama means death. The yamas are essentially the way we bring about compassionate death to our ego. In the Upanishads, they have been referred to as the "restraints." There are five yamas: *ahimsa:* nonviolence; *satya:* truth in word and thought; *asteya:* nonstealing; *brahmacharya:* conscious choice-making regarding sexual behavior (traditionally brahmacharya is associated with celibacy or *"thou shalt not have sex";* I prefer to see it as

"let us pay attention to the relationship choices we make");
and *aparigraha:* absence of greed.

2. *NIYAMA:* PERSONAL OBSERVANCES (CHOICES)

The niyamas are the prescribed actions and personal
observances that reflect the internal dialogue of conscious
people. If the yamas are the *Universal* DO NOTs, the niyamas are the *Personal* DOs. These observances include practices and teachings for making the most evolutionary personal choices in life. Historically, the niyamas are: *shaucha:*
cleanliness of body and mind; *santosha:* contentment with
what one has; *tapas:* austerity; *svādhyāya:* study of the Vedic
scriptures to better know the Self; and *ishvarapranidhana:*
surrender to God. Tradition dictates that these are serious
observances to master.

3. *ASANA:* BODY POSTURES OR POSES

The asana is the intimate relationship between our
personal and extended bodies.

4. *PRANAYAMA:* BREATHING EXERCISES AND CONTROL OF PRANA (VITAL ENERGY)

Pranayama represents the awareness and integration of
the rhythms, seasons, and cycles of our life.

5. *PRATYAHARA:* CONTROL OF THE SENSES

By withdrawing from our five senses, we can tune
in to our subtle sensory experiences—seeing beyond our
eyes, hearing without our ears, smelling without our nose,
tasting without our mouth, and feeling without our body.

6. *DHARANA:* CONCENTRATION AND CULTIVATING INNER PERCEPTUAL AWARENESS

This is the very first step in the process of meditating: attention. Dharana is the evolutionary expression of attention and intention. This is an active practice of refining one's ability to maintain a single point of focus.

7. *DHYANA:* MEDITATION

The second step in the process of meditating—once attention has been mastered—is dhyana. Patanjali referred to this as meditation, essentially when the act of concentrating becomes perfected and there is no longer the need to try or do in order to connect one to the pure being state of consciousness. It's the junction between the personal and the universal aspects of our being—the non-dualistic state of consciousness.

8. *SAMADHI:* UNION WITH THE DIVINE

Samadhi is the third piece of the meditative experience once dharana (refined attention) and dhyana (meditation) have been mastered. Similar to the mastering of metta and samatha bhavanas before one enters the realm of vipassana, once your attention and meditation skills have been cultivated, samadhi is one-ness—the progressive expansion of the Self.

Yoga is a rich, broad, beautiful fabric that weaves through every aspect of existence . . . our physical bodies, our environment, our mind, intellect, ego, emotional being, our daily interactions, and our spiritual Self—our soul. Yoga connects them all through the practice of the eight limbs. The next time the word "yoga" flows into your awareness, expand your perception beyond the concept of asana to include the other seven limbs. Then you'll truly be practicing yoga on and off the mat.

Although the physical and emotional benefits of a daily yoga practice are well documented and are a magnificent foundation for right livelihood and a solid meditation practice, the practice of asana always keeps us in activity.

Even when practicing the Seven Spiritual Laws of Yoga, a spiritual and meditative type of yoga, the body-centric nature of the practice still keeps us in activity. It is only in sitting meditation that we truly disconnect from activity to experience stillness and silence. Meditation creates the passive state of restful awareness—the pure experience in which we are neither in the past nor in the future but are solidly immersed in the present moment.

Sensory meditations can help you feel.

CHAPTER NINE

SECRETS OF
BUDDHIST MEDITATION

"There is no need for temples, no need for complicated philosophies. My brain and my heart are my temples; my philosophy is kindness."

— HIS HOLINESS THE 14TH DALAI LAMA

Prince Siddhartha Gautama, commonly referred to as the Buddha or "one who is awake," is said to have lived approximately 2,500 years ago. At the age of 29, the young Siddhartha ventured out beyond the palace walls for the very first time and witnessed a whole new world—one of suffering, aging, illness, birth, and death. This led him to choose a path of poverty, withdrawal from all worldly desires, self-denial of earthly pleasures, and self-starvation. He then dedicated himself to a life of austerity, asceticism, and meditation. Of course this only created a very thin and austere meditator.

One day when he was close to the point of death through self-starvation, a young girl offered him a bowl of rice, and he accepted it. At that moment, he realized that severe austerity would not lead to enlightenment. From then on, Siddhartha encouraged people to follow a path he called "the middle way"—devotion to moderation between the extremes of self-indulgence and self-mortification. His followers became disengaged, believing he had lost his focus and lost his mind. So they left him.

That night he sat under a pipal tree, meditating in the north Indian town of Bodhgaya, vowing not to stop until he had attained Truth. He practiced *anapanasati,* a meditation practice in which you focus your awareness on breathing in and out. After meditating for

49 days, he experienced enlightenment at the age of 35. From that point on, he was known as the Buddha, which means "One who is awake." Stories are told that because Buddha had no witnesses to the enlightenment that came to him during that meditation, he moved his right hand down from his lap and touched the ground beneath his folded knee so the earth could be his witness. This is why you often see statues and paintings of Buddha meditating with his right hand reaching down from his knee.

After achieving enlightenment, the Buddha spent four months each year with his monks, discussing and practicing his teachings. After his death, his followers shared these teachings, at first by continuing the oral tradition and then by writing them down. Buddhism has flourished in many areas of the world, and its philosophy and practices have become increasingly popular in the Western world as people recognize their value, wisdom, and practicality.

What Is It All About?

Much has been written about Siddhartha by authors ranging from Hermann Hesse to Deepak Chopra, and you don't have to be a Buddhist to practice Buddhist meditations. At no point during a Buddhist meditation is it required or requested that you pray to the Buddha or believe in the teachings of the Buddha. In fact, all Buddhist meditations are about attention and mindfulness, not a person or a deity. Buddha can even help you get closer to Jesus Christ.

The core of Buddhist teachings is what is known as the Four Noble Truths:

1. Suffering, or *dukkha,* is a predominant experience in life.

2. The root of suffering, or *dukkha samudaya,* is clinging to desires.

3. The end of suffering, or *dukkha nirodha,* comes about through ceasing to cling.

4. Freedom from suffering can be attained by practicing *dukkha nirodha gamini patipada magga,* known as the Noble Eightfold Path, which describes eight ways to end suffering, as detailed by Siddhartha.

The Noble Eightfold Path is a practical guideline for an individual's spiritual, moral, and mental development. Buddha instructed that if you live each day with these eight characteristics as your guiding principles, you will transcend the conditioned attachments, illusions, and delusions that create suffering in your life. Following these guidelines leads to a deeper understanding of all things, which includes the expansion of:

- **Wisdom** through 1) right view; 2) right intention
- **Moral conduct** through 3) right speech; 4) right action; 5) right livelihood
- **Mental development** through 6) right effort; 7) right mindfulness; and 8) right concentration

According to Buddhism, practicing the guidelines of the Eightfold Path in our daily life while having a deep understanding of the Four Noble Truths is how one attains a higher level of existence and ultimately reaches Nirvana, a state of union with all things—Buddhism's version of one-ness.

Practicing a Buddhist meditation is simply resonating with the vibrations of the universe through the guidance of one of the most amazing teachers to have ever lived and connecting to his traits of peaceful coexistence and unconditional love, as well as expressing compassion and loving-kindness to others. This would seem to support the tenets of Christianity, Islam, Judaism, Hinduism, Jainism, Mormonism, Sikhism, Taoism, Confucianism, Sufism, even atheism . . . and even in the most fundamental or detached expressions of devotion to a higher power.

The Bhavanas

The primary purpose of Buddhist meditation is to train the mind to be still. The Buddhist term for meditation is *bhavana,* or "mental cultivation," and the three most well-known bhavanas are: metta (loving-kindness), samatha (tranquility), and vipassana (insight). Let's explore each of these.

1. METTA—LOVING-KINDNESS

In *metta bhavana,* you concentrate on sending out loving-kindness to all living beings. In the metta meditative exercises, I like to start with directing thoughts of benevolence, love, and compassion *inward.* Although self-directed loving-kindness was never specifically instructed by the Buddha, I have found that starting the meditation this way quickly engages and empowers me by providing a very clear object of attention. Master metta practitioners have assured me that other Buddhist writings imply that it is an appropriate start to the practice. After you have radiated loving-kindness inward, you move from the easiest to the more difficult. Using your own well-being or your heart as a point of reference for gradually radiating loving-kindness outward, you direct it first to those you deeply respect, such as your most revered teachers or life guides. Next, you radiate loving-kindness to your loved ones, and then to your friends, and then acquaintances, then to those you don't even know. And as you continue to expand your circle of loving-kindness, you direct loving-kindness to your "enemies" and finally toward all beings on the planet.

I have found metta meditation to be a very nourishing practice. Both first-time meditators and seasoned meditators appreciate its simple sweetness. I recommend that you take your time; do it very slowly. Start with 15 minutes, get comfortable there, and then see if you can stretch it to 30 minutes—the perfect amount of time to receive the optimal benefits of a practice.

2. Samatha—Tranquility

Samatha bhavana is about single-mindedness of purpose. The meditator focuses on one object or action, such as breathing or a drishti point. This meditation cultivates your abilities of concentration. Samatha bhavana practitioners believe that by concentrating on just one thing for a period of time, the mind will become still . . . stilled to the point of calmness and *tranquility* . . . hence the name samatha. This practice is thought to prepare the mind for the third type of bhavana, *vipassana,* or insight meditation. Master Buddhist meditators advise spending years cultivating the mind through samatha bhavana before moving on to vipassana—the more advanced bhavana. Yet, as American Buddhism has flourished over the past 40 years, attention on samatha bhavana has withered and vipassana has thrived.

3. Vipassana—Insight

Now that the mind has been made calm through samatha bhavana, it is ready to be trained further through the practice of *vipassana bhavana,* in which you are mindful of all your thoughts and feelings and witness them with detachment until you have the experience of insight into the truth of your life. When you experience thoughts, sounds, or physical sensations, you don't react to them. Rather, you stay present with them as they occur and witness them with no judgment. You simply let them *be.*

Vipassana is known as the meditation practice that the Buddha practiced. I find vipassana to be very simple and inclusive. I practiced it for several years just because of its ease and found the practice to be a nurturing and gentle form of meditation. I recommend that you experience vipassana at some point in your life, but unless you desire to explore the first two bhavanas, you won't experience the true depth of that beautiful practice. I skipped from metta bhavana right to vipassana. My impatience did not serve me, as I never experienced the depth of one-ness nor the post-meditation richness in my life that Primordial Sound Meditation now affords me. Had I spent a few years first cultivating my samatha practice, I probably would have had a greater appreciation for vipassana.

Each month as I connect with thousands of people around the world exploring meditation, I am always touched by the sweet energy emitted by those who walk in the path of the Buddha. Not necessarily those who claim they are Buddhists, but those who practice mindfulness on a daily basis regardless of their "official" philosophy or religion. They live their lives as an expression of an open heart. They practice loving-kindness without expectation of acknowledgment or recognition; they are gentle beings and, therefore, create gentleness in their world. They are less caught up in drama, because they worry less about the past or future and stay in the moment . . . they walk this earth with softness, sweetness, and compassion. They are a pleasure to be around; they are truly loving-kindness embodied. I learn so much about myself and about the world from them. Most often, these people tell me that they are not necessarily Buddhists but that they have a daily heart opening or meditation practice such as metta bhavana. When you fill your heart with loving-kindness for an hour each day, it ultimately begins to flow out of you, regardless of the depth or emptiness of your abyss.

Buddhist meditations can help you be more mindful.

CHAPTER TEN

Secrets of Mantra Meditation

*"A human being is a part of the whole, called
by us Universe, a part limited in time and space.
He experiences himself, his thoughts and feeling as
something separated from the rest—a kind of optical
delusion of his consciousness. This delusion is a kind of
prison for us, restricting us to our personal desires and to
affection for a few persons nearest to us. Our task must be
to free ourselves from this prison by widening our circle
of compassion to embrace all living creatures and
the whole of nature in its beauty."*

— ALBERT EINSTEIN

My current mantra meditation practice is one born of my lifelong spiritual voyage, which began in my mother's womb. She believed in the concept of the unbounded universal self, and she and I explored it in many ways throughout my youth before her body died. I still feel a very deep spiritual connection to her even 30 years after she left this earthly plane. She was always open to new teachings and guided me to expand my reference point beyond the traditional religious, philosophical, and spiritual tutelage I received. That encouraged me to explore and appreciate the rituals and deeper philosophies woven through many other cultures and schools of devotion.

My comfort with a poly-philosophical approach to our existence has allowed me to embrace the Torah as well as the Vedas, Christ consciousness, Islam's mystical Sufism, Osho's Taoism, Guru Nanak's Sikhism, the loving-kindness of Buddha's compassionate teachings, and the universality of religious science. I see them all as different paths to the same outcome, alternate narratives of the same archetypal story, all resonating the same frequency and common theme: to live a life of purpose, peace, compassion, love, and fulfillment.

Studying and practicing this blend of teachings has helped me transcend the many traumas, struggles, and challenges that I have experienced in my life. It has helped me make peace with much of the pain of my past and the potential-turbulences that I swim through each day. It has helped me to move into the present and help others find deeper fulfillment in their lives. It has taught me that I can't undo the past . . . I can't unring the bell . . . I can't unhurt those I have wounded—but I can make different choices in this moment to right my past wrongs, to say now what I couldn't or didn't say then, to make amends for past misdeeds, to listen now to what I couldn't hear then, to add sweetness to the lives of new people in my life in the same way I have brought pain into the lives of those in my past, to bring closure to the past in my heart and in my mind even when I am unable to do it in this physical world, and to take responsibility for my feelings, my interpretations, and my dreams.

What Is in a Mantra?

The traditional image of a meditator is someone sitting cross-legged with eyes closed and their hands resting on their knees, with thumbs and index fingers touching to form a circle as they chant the sound Om. That chanting of Om is what's called the chanting of a mantra, and if you remember all the way back to Chapter 1, the word "mantra" comes from two Sanskrit words: *man,* which means "mind," and *tra,* which means "vehicle" or "instrument." So your mantra is your mind vehicle . . . your mind instrument. It is a tool to transport the mind from a state of activity to one of stillness and silence. We get the words **"train," "travel,"** and **"transporta-tion"** from the Sanskrit root *tra.* Most mantras are comprised of the 50 letters of the Sanskrit alphabet. Mantras can consist of a single letter, a syllable or string of syllables, a word, or a whole sentence.

Typically, most mantras are sounds, syllables, or vibrations that don't necessarily have a meaning. Their value lies in their vibrational quality, not in any meaning that humans, society, culture, or civilization has placed on them over the last few thousand years. For this reason, they go beyond the state of human existence on this planet. And they take you deeper, because they are vibrations that have existed since the dawn of creation.

The Hymn of the Universe

Om, often referred to as the hymn of the universe, is the oldest mantra sacred to Hindus, Buddhists, and Jains. Om is considered the ultimate vibration, because it contains every vibration that has ever existed and every vibration that will ever exist. Just as white light contains all the colors of the spectrum, Om contains every sound in the vibrational spectrum—even those we can't hear with our ears. One of the clearest visual representations of this is on the cover of Pink Floyd's album *Dark Side of the Moon*. It shows the white light coming into a prism and all the colors of the spectrum coming out the other side. The same could be said for Om; it's the white light of sound.

Historically, Om is first mentioned in the 12 verses of the ancient Vedic text the Mandukya Upanishads, which explains the three basic states of consciousness: waking, sleeping, and dreaming. In its original spelling and pronunciation, *Aum* (pronounced "ahh-uhh-mmm") is a blending of those three states of consciousness into the one-ness of three distinct syllables: A, U, and M. These three vibrations also represent the three stages of our known existence: birth, life, and death.

The vibration *a* (pronounced "ahh," like the sound you make opening your mouth for the doctor) represents the waking state and the beginning of all things. Just as the letter A is the first letter of most every alphabet—the first letter of the Rig Veda, the Koran, Homer's *Odyssey,* even the first word of the New Testament—the vibration A heralds creation . . . the beginning. Vedic sages refer to it as the *A-kara,* and it represents the realm of form and shape—the physical realm.

The vibration *u* (pronounced "oo") is referred to as the *U-kara* and represents the dream state, the realm that is devoid of form or shape—the ethereal realms of air, water, fire, dreams— ever-changing aspects of the formless world around us.

The vibration *m* is known as the *Ma-kara,* which represents the state of deep sleep . . . neither form or formless like the other two realms but beyond shape or shapelessness . . . the realm of consciousness in hibernation, waiting to unfold.

In Sanskrit grammar, when the letters A and U are combined in writing, they are translated as the letter O. That is why we so often see Om written instead of Aum. Over thousands of years, the writing of Aum has taken a backseat to Om, and that has led to Om being the sound that is most often chanted by both Western students and teachers of yoga, meditation, and Vedanta. In India, where people have a greater familiarity with Sanskrit from daily prayer, the sound is still pronounced Aum.

When the three individual vibrations are combined, a fourth vibration is created, like a chord in music made up of individual notes. Aum (pronounced "ahhh-uhhh-mmmm") represents the fourth state of consciousness—transcendent consciousness, or *turiya* . . . what we call enlightenment or one-ness. In Hinduism, it's the unity of the divine made up of its three components: *Brahma*—creation, *Vishnu*—preservation, and *Shiva*—destruction and rebirth. The chanting of the mantra Om heralds our universality, which is why we usually chant Om before and/or after meditation and yoga practice, and when we read sacred, ancient texts.

By repeating a vibration or sound over and over, it will become part of your physiology; it will become your mind; it will become *you.* It will lose all meaning, all definition, and all relevance. There will be no separation between you and the vibration that is resonating right now.

OM—THE HYMN OF THE UNIVERSE

This is the Sanskrit symbol for the vibration Om. The large curve on the lower left represents the material world of the waking state; the smaller curve on the upper-left represents the state of deep sleep. The curve on the right that extends to the right from the intersection of the two left curves represents the dream state—that tender line between waking and sleeping. The dot at the very top is akin to the dot (or bindu) in the center of the sri yantra discussed at length in Chapter 5, "Secrets of Visual Meditation," and represents the universe in all its abundance. This state is often referred to as *turiya* (pronounced "tour-i-yah"), a Sanskrit word for "absolute consciousness," "the universe," or "one-ness." And the curved line under the bindu represents maya, the illusion of existence that separates our bodymind from one-ness and must be transcended for us to return to the whole. Ommmmm!

Mantras can be uttered aloud or silently. When a mantra is chanted out loud, it is intended to concentrate, intensify, and expand consciousness. Ancient Vedic texts maintain that a whispered mantra is a thousand times more beneficial than a spoken one, and a silent mantra is a thousand times more powerful than a whispered one.

Meditating on Om

We can meditate right now using the mantra Om. Say it out loud and feel the vibration *a-u-m* as it is birthed, then sustains, and then dies out as you purse your lips. Now let's whisper it. *Om.* And now begin repeating it silently to yourself. *Om, Om, Om, Om.* To practice any type of mantra meditation, close your eyes and silently repeat the mantra over and over. When you notice that you have drifted away from the mantra to thoughts in your mind, sounds in the environment, or sensations in your physical body, gently drift back to the mantra. It will get louder and fainter, faster and slower; it will even become jumbled, distorted, and inaudible. However the mantra changes, simply keep repeating it, and when you notice you've drifted away just gently drift back. Back and forth and back and forth again. Gently surrender to the back and forth.

Let's try it for a few moments right now. Just for a few moments. But first take a deep breath in through your nostrils and hold it for a moment and then slowly let it out. Do that again. And then close your eyes and begin silently repeating *Om.*

Now, let's meditate for a few moments.

How did that feel? What did you feel?

Mantras with Meaning

Early in Vedic history, teachers began categorizing mantras as either meaningful or meaningless. Meaningless mantras are simply sounds used for their vibrational quality. They don't have a particular meaning or correlation. Meaningful mantras, on the other hand, inherently contain some intention or meaning that is determined by the culture and language in which they arise, as well as a personal meaning. These mantras both connect the reciter with a particular intention and serve as a meditation vehicle, helping to awaken a specific state of consciousness. Examples of meaningful mantras include the ancient sutras known in Sanskrit as the *mahavakyas,* or "master sayings." Deepak Chopra detailed these seven mahavakyas in his best-selling classic *The Spontaneous Fulfillment of Desire as*:

- Aham brahmasmi—I am the universe
- Tat tvam asi—I am that
- Sat chit ananda—truth, knowledge, bliss
- San kalpa—the power of the subtle intention
- Moksha—I am emotionally free
- Shiva-shakti—awaken your divine masculine-feminine energy
- Ritam—flow to the rhythm of the universe

The mahavakyas are drawn from the ancient Vedic texts known as the Upanishads. And as a devoted student of these teachings, a highlight of my Chopra Center tenure was teaching Vedanta alongside Deepak and David at the SynchroDestiny manifestation workshops. For a solid decade, until SynchroDestiny was retired in early 2012, thousands of attendees learned to manifest their deepest desires in accordance with the mahavakyas, receiving life guidance filled with reverence, brilliance, and integrity from these two masters.

But there are many sutras beyond the mahavakyas, and I encourage you to find one that feels comfortable—one that has a meaning with which you connect, as well as a vibrational quality with which you resonate. Aham brahmasmi is one of my favorites. It feels comfortable and empowering, and on a vibrational level, it is soothing.

Mantras Used for Their Vibrational Quality

Most forms of mantra meditation use a mantra or mind instrument to disconnect us from the activity around us—the thoughts, sounds, and physical sensations that are a part of every moment we are alive. In contrast with vipassana meditation, where practitioners put their attention on these activities of the bodymind, mantra meditation uses the repetition of a meaningless syllable, syllables, or vibrations to disconnect us from those same activities. Our present-moment awareness is on the mantra's vibration, not the many other possible activities of the moment and after consistent silent repetition—it becomes the sole object of our attention. We have between 60,000 and 80,000 thoughts each day. That's about a thought every second and a simultaneous awareness of meaning that leads to activity. By repeating a *meaningless* syllable or syllables, such as Om, the meditator can disconnect from meaning and slip into a space between thoughts, where there is no activity. By repeating something that is meaningless over and over and over again, an open, undefined space washes over every aspect of you—beyond your labels, beyond your definitions, beyond your meanings and understandings—and into the space of one-ness.

Your mantra is your hyperlink to the nonlocal domain.

The Power of Mantra

Once this space of stillness and silence becomes you, you truly detach from thoughts in the mind, sounds in the environment, and physical sensations in the body. Your heart rate slows . . . your breathing slows . . . the past drifts away . . . the ongoing speculation about the future ceases. There is a subtle awareness of moving from activity to stillness; thoughts and sounds pass through you instead of being received and processed by you. A lightness of being flows into you. The concept of you expands from a breathing human being to a silent observer to a unified being, seeing the sacred in every face, flower, and object around you. Ultimately, you merge into everything without distinction.

There is one-ness . . . there is unity . . . there is stillness . . . silence . . . bliss . . . no separation between anything . . . your pure unconditioned self.

This is "it"—what is commonly referred to as "being in the gap." And the beauty is that you can't know you're there; it's beyond space and time. You stay in this higher state of consciousness until your body pulls you out of it by drifting back into activity as your awareness drifts to a thought, a sound, or a physical sensation—and you flow out of one-ness and back to duality.

At the moment you begin to drift out of the stillness and silence, you start to apply meaning to the moment. That is when you realize you were in "the gap"; it's always after the fact . . . never while you're there. It is at that moment you recognize the difference . . . the separation between *that* and *this,* or the duality of our individual local existence and our universal nonlocal one. Meaning comes back into your awareness. You can't recognize the gap while you are in it, because you are not separate from it. It's like a fish swimming through the ocean, unaware that it's in water, fully immersed and integrated into the ocean during its entire life until it chooses to leap out of its liquid realm into the air—then it truly realizes separation.

It is at this moment—as you become aware of your thoughts again—that you drift back into the realm of meaning and activity. As you drift out of the stillness, you become aware of the mantra or perhaps a new thought, a sound, or a physical sensation. This is normal, common, expected; this is part of the meditation. But regardless of where you find yourself, just gently drift back to the effortless repetition of the mantra. Keep drifting back and forth.

This is meditation plain and simple . . . drifting ever so gently back and forth between the object of attention (the mantra) to activity (thoughts, sounds, and physical sensations) . . . and then back again to the mantra. Don't torture yourself; don't try to control anything. But as soon as you become aware you are no longer repeating the mantra (which is the most common experience), just gently drift back to it. The repetition of the mantra is effortless, like mist rising off a lake at dawn. Any more effort and you're working way too hard.

There are millions of mantras, because they are sounds or myriad combinations of sounds. And they are used for many different purposes—devotional, spiritual, healing, mystical, material—and in many different ways—silently repeated, chanted, whispered, sung in chorus, and read by a leader and responded to. I believe in the power of the mantra, and almost any mantra used with the right intention in a daily practice can take one from a very personal constricted state of existence to higher states of consciousness, including more expanded and universal states.

USING A BIJA

The word *bija* (pronounced "bee-jah") means "seed" in Sanskrit and as such, is a metaphor for the cause or origin of something. Thousands of years ago, the *rishis,* or seers, in what is now the Indian subcontinent identified what they believed to be the original sounds of nature. They called them bija sounds or seed syllables. The oldest of these bija sounds—Om—is first referenced in the ancient Vedic text known as the Upanishads. Since then, these powerful bija sounds have been used as mantras because they are organic, pure, universal vibrations.

In the late '60s and early '70s, meditation was reintroduced to the masses, creating one of the most powerful shifts in consciousness on the planet. With legendary Beatle George Harrison leading the way and the other members of Sergeant Pepper's Lonely Hearts Club Band following the path, millions around the world, and especially in the United States and Western Europe, tapped into mantra meditation as a way of life.

Many of my friends, colleagues, and students had the honor of learning to meditate with a personal mantra in the 1970s under the tutelage of Maharishi Mahesh Yogi, the founder of the Transcendental Meditation (TM) movement and technique of meditation. They were taught to use a bija to disconnect them from activity.

When used as a mantra in meditation, seed sounds can connect you directly to source. The value of using a bija is that it's not a word that has meaning; it's simply a vibration—a vibration that has existed forever—a primordial sound. The beauty of a primordial sound is that even if we give it meaning, since it was never intended to have meaning, its vibrational quality is what holds our attention, which is then drifted away from things that have meaning.

Primordial Sound Meditation

The mantra technique that has worked for me for many years, and the one that I have taught most of my students over the past decade, is Primordial Sound Meditation. It was first taught to me in 2002 by Ravi Meher, a meditation instructor then certified by Chopra Center University, who flew from London to the States to teach me and six other students our personal mantra and the ins and outs of Primordial Sound Meditation through four sessions over three days. I believe it has altered my DNA over the past ten years; it has taken me deeper than any other meditation technique and provided amazing experiences along the way. It has sharpened my clarity, provided tranquility, released my stresses, strengthened my understanding of existence, lessened my potential for anxiety, offered thousands of insights, exploded many of my limiting beliefs, expanded my capacity for compassion and forgiveness, profoundly connected me to source, and given me immeasurable gifts that I am unable to articulate.

I have experienced amazingly powerful results from this technique over the past ten years by simply practicing twice each day for 30 minutes each session . . . typically once in the very early morning and once in the late afternoon or evening.

Your primordial sound is the vibration the universe was making at the moment you passed from the unmanifest into the manifest and came into this world of form and phenomena.

Primordial Sound Meditation is a mantra-based meditation technique that dates back thousands of years and incorporates primordial bija sounds—the very first sounds of nature, the earliest primal sounds of the planet, the most subtle sounds of the universe that existed at the dawn of creation, before there was industry, before electricity was harnessed, before there was language, before there was meaning. As a basic sound of nature, a primordial sound carries the energetic vibration inherent in the atmosphere of a particular place at a specific moment in time. In the late 1990s, Deepak Chopra and David Simon rebirthed this ancient practice with the blessing of the Shankaracharya, the modern-day preserver of these ancient teachings located in northern India. One of my first roles when I began serving at the Chopra Center was to oversee the development of a cutting-edge computer model that calculated a person's primordial sound mantra.

Meditating to Your Primordial Sound

There are hundreds of thousands of meditators around the world who practice Primordial Sound Meditation. There are approximately 108 primordial sounds in this school of meditation, and they are raw, pure, untouched, and universal. Each Primordial Sound meditator uses a unique sound, or mantra, that reflects the vibration or the atmospheric quality of the universe at the moment of his or her birth. The vibration is calculated based on the place, date, and time of a person's birth. This information is then correlated to the changing vibrations of the universe that were written down in Sanskrit thousands of years ago. A Vedic mathematics program then calculates the vibration from the 108 possibilities. Once identified, that vibration is merged into several other vibrations, including other bija sounds, to create an individual's personal mantra. Once you are taught your primordial sound mantra, you repeat it silently during your meditation practice to move you more easily into stillness and silence.

It's pretty powerful to meditate using the sound that the universe was making at the moment you passed from the unmanifest into the manifest. It's also very powerful to know that the exact same alignment between the earth and the moon that existed at the moment you were born is the exact same relationship that existed between the earth and the moon 5,000 years ago, when this vibration was first heard and written down. We humans come and go every hundred years, but the sun, the moon, the earth, and the planets have been signposts of the galaxy for more than 15 billion years . . . 15 billion!

That may not sound like a lot, considering that our government spends a *billion* dollars every few minutes, but humans have only walked the earth for the past 150,000 years, with the first civilizations developing only 10,000 years ago. That's right. We've all been hanging out here together on this third rock from the sun for only 10,000 years—a mere 100 centuries. The wisdom of the universe is vast, timeless, and so beyond what we could ever comprehend. The sounds that have existed since the first insects, worms, fish, birds, lizards, frogs, dinosaurs, wolves, dolphins, horses, apes, whales, and humans first drew breath are expressions of that wisdom . . . the sounds of existence, an existence that has flowed for billions of years. And that vibration—*your* vibration—the atmospheric quality that was defined by the infinite laws of nature has been resonating for billions of years . . . since forever. The bija sound you are taught as part of your mantra is the very first vibration you heard upon being born. This vibration heralded your entry into this realm. This was the vibrational seed of your life's trajectory

This isn't a commentary on when life begins. Rather, these teachings celebrate the moment we truly became individuated. The moment we first heard sound through air instead of through amniotic fluid . . . and the first moment we were truly physically separated from anyone else as our umbilical cord was cut. So the fact that my sound—my mantra—is individual to me makes it very special on an egoistic level. Knowing that my mantra is different from most other people means we are all using a somewhat customized personal energy to tap into the timeless energy of the collective consciousness. It's the individual and the universal existing all at once—the gap—one-ness. We use our own individual vehicle to take us to the place where we are all one! Your Primordial Sound Meditation instructor can teach you this ancient practice, sharing the rich history, your primordial sound, how to practically apply meditation to your daily life, and then explore higher states of consciousness with you. Find a teacher at **davidji.com.**

How Is Primordial Sound Meditation Unique?

One day, one of my students of five years visited me to discuss her meditation practice. On returning home from a Buddhist meditation retreat, she had immersed in a daily vipassana bhavana practice and let go of her mantra practice. Weeks had passed, and although she had a sense of peacefulness in her life, she sensed that something had shifted . . . something had changed. She had practiced Primordial Sound Meditation for almost five years and experienced higher states of consciousness—cosmic consciousness, divine consciousness . . . even unity consciousness on one occasion when she was on retreat—but for the past month, as she practiced mindfulness, she had drifted away from those higher states of consciousness in her life and wanted to reconnect to them. I celebrate meditation in all its forms, so it didn't matter to me what type of meditation she did, as long as she was finding it added value to her life.

She insisted that this questioning wasn't about which meditation technique was more effective but rather, her understanding of what was actually happening within her by shifting from a mantra practice to a mindfulness practice. I had journeyed in the other direction—from a vipassana practice to a mantra meditation practice—and my experiences had gotten deeper and more powerful over time.

There is no right or wrong meditation technique; neither is better than the other. It depends on what you are needing or looking for at a given time. Over the last decade, I have found mantra meditation to be a powerful tool for me based on what I was seeking in my life. My experiences of unity consciousness that flicker within me throughout my day have transformed me in so many ways. My connection to source feels deeper now than it did when I practiced mindfulness meditation. Yet once in a while, it feels great to surrender to mindfulness meditation or any other meditative practice.

In 2012, I was invited to record 40 days of meditations for a free online program known as the Winter Feast for the Soul. The "feast" is based on the Sufi poet Jelaluddin Rumi's quote, "What nine months does for the embryo, forty early mornings will do for your growing awareness."

Most religions reference a 40-day transformational experience as well. There are many biblical and historical references to 40 days: Moses prayed for 40 days on Mt. Sinai; David and Goliath fought twice a day for 40 days; the ancient Egyptians packed the bodies of the dead for 40 days before mummifying them; the prophet Muhammad fasted and practiced abstinence for 40 days; Buddha meditated for 40 to 49 days under the Bodhi tree before experiencing enlightenment; Jesus fasted in the wilderness for 40 days, which is why Lent is 40 days. Simply Googling "40 days" turns up hundreds of references to this 40-day connection.

The Winter Feast for the Soul heralded that connection. Each day, meditators from all over the world—at every level of experience and practice—logged on, turned up their speakers, and journeyed with one of the many types of meditation offered for 40 days in a row. Each day, you had seven choices including a Sufi meditation, a Rabbi leading a Kabalistic meditation, Christian contemplative prayer, a Sikh meditation, vipassana bhavana, even meditations for children led by the renowned kid's yoga teacher Jodi Komitor. While I led the 40 meditations in the category of Vedanta/nondenominational, each meditation was followed by a metta moment—an act of loving-kindness that each of us could flow into the world that day. The beauty of the feast for me was that I was able to merge Vedanta meditation and metta bhavana into a seamless experience, allowing the online meditator to feel the union as well. It is my intention to continue to participate in the Winter Feast for the Soul. More than 10,000 daily meditators journeyed with us for 10 minutes of a lesson and then 30 minutes of stillness and silence, followed by our metta moment, where we all shared an act of loving-kindness. Can you imagine the ripple effect of this sweet silence spanning the globe as meditators in every time zone logged on together for 40 days? The power of the collective is profound and for 40 days thousands of us shared it on a universal journey of one-ness. Cultivating mindfulness and sharing acts of metta is a beautiful daily practice, and I recommend it to everyone—no matter what your style of meditation is. And while daily vipassana bhavana offered me the experience of mindfulness and present-moment awareness for the time I practiced it, Primordial Sound Meditation offers me a true sense of one-ness, or non-duality, between the local domain of the here and now and the nonlocal realm of the universe.

The philosophy that explains the concept of one-ness most articulately is known in Sanskrit as *Advaita* (pronounced "ad-viy-ta") or non-duality. It was first popularized by Adi Shankara, a 9th-century sage who, at the age of 12, was one of the most brilliant translators of Vedanta and laid it all out in his timeless classic *The Crest Jewel of Discrimination*. Almost 1,400 years later, millions still find rich value in his teachings and translations. In our century, Advaita's essence was most effectively rebirthed and popularized in the early 1970s by the Maharishi Mahesh Yogi. And for the past 35 years, this non-dualistic school of thought has been poetically and practically articulated by Deepak Chopra and David Simon in books, lectures, satsangs, and workshops. For the past decade, these two teachers have generously shared these non-dualistic philosophies and complementary healing methodologies with the world, and I have had the good fortune to be there in person right at their side to witness, download, immerse in, and integrate the timeless wisdom into my being.

But back to my story. My student was now at a meditation crossroads, and my concern was that she would stop meditating altogether, because she was conflicted between styles. I needed a way to articulate the difference in the two styles to her while "giving her permission" to choose either, even if it wasn't my style. I saw this as an opportunity to connect with one of my teachers for guidance.

One of the greatest gifts I have received over the years has been sitting 20 feet from David Simon during much of his 13-year tenure as medical director of the Chopra Center. In addition to being close confidantes in our personal lives, several times each day, he and I would pop into each others' offices to spend quality time exploring and contemplating life, death, love, the Vedas, the daily workings of the Chopra Center, family, enlightenment, healing, a TV show, reincarnation, cosmic consciousness, or a funny story. Sometimes it was for just a few moments and sometimes longer. David was in the middle of writing his classic bestseller on emotional healing—*Free to Love, Free to Heal*—when I knocked on his door. I stood in his doorway and explained my dilemma. What I thought would be a two-minute conversation on vipassana turned into a two-hour mini-meditation retreat. He stopped writing and disconnected completely from what he was doing, becoming totally present with my issue.

He gazed into my eyes and asked me a few questions about my day. He told me a story about his dad and then belly-laughed as he remembered a conversation he had with one of his daughters. He pulled books off the shelf and read me passages from an Osho book on Sufism, several verses from the Bhagavad Gita, and excerpts from a meditation study in a medical journal he was reading. He told me a few jokes and remembered he had two pieces of 85 percent cacao organic dark chocolate, which we slipped into our mouths and then sat with our eyes closed, letting the melting nectar trickle down our throats.

Then we meditated using our primordial sound mantras, and after about 20 minutes of the practice, he whispered, "Aham brahmasmi—I am the universe." Then we chanted Om together. As we let the vibration settle into silence, he opened a book and read a few poems from the great Sufi poet Hafiz. Then together, we responsively read sutras on one-ness from the Yoga Vasistha. He would read a sutra out loud as I listened with my eyes closed; then I repeated it back to him. This verbal back-and-forth ritual is known as responsive reading, and as we rocked various versions of one-ness back and forth to each other, the sutras melted into words, the words into syllables, the syllables into sounds, the sounds into vibrations, and the vibrations into a single vibration that then melted into our essence. The unity of that moment seemed to last lifetimes, as all of our words merged into an intoxicating blend of universal vibrations and then into silence.

When we had concluded our present-moment experience, hours had passed, and I was in a state of profound clarity. I stood, hugged him, and with tears of mirth trickling down my cheeks,

I walked out of his office. I looked back over my shoulder as he slowly swiveled his chair back to his computer and drifted his fingers back to his keyboard. He rhetorically asked in the softest of whispers, "Does that answer your question?" as he unfolded a sweet, knowing grin.

Almost as if sleepwalking, I stepped back into my office and sat in silence with my assistant Tiffany. She intuitively closed the door behind us and then sat in similar silence as if entrained by the vibration I had carried from David's office into ours. We locked eyes for a few moments and then experienced a quick mutual rush of unity consciousness. I don't know how much time passed as the stillness and silence progressively became the room. I closed my eyes and then opened them a few minutes later. I rested my fingers on my keyboard as if in a trance to upload what I had just experienced as I integrated it into my being.

Then I wrote, "The value of mantra meditation is in quieting the mind and awakening the silent witness. This not only awakens our knowledge of witnessing awareness (as does vipassana), but also awakens a certain understanding that even the witness alone is incomplete. The process in which the witness, the process of witnessing, and that which is witnessed are unified is the goal of mantra meditation, which takes one into the gap of stillness and silence. As David Simon so eloquently taught me with our silence, it is the merging of this witness (known as rishi), the process of witnessing (known as devata), and that which is witnessed (known as chandas)—essentially the fusion of the observer, the act of observing, and the object of observation into the union . . . the yoga of life. Vipassana is useful in the first stage of becoming more mindful but cannot lead to unity. Advaita fulfills the intention of vipassana, but vipassana cannot fulfill the intention of non-duality."

Later that afternoon, awakened to a crystallized clarity, I met with my student and encouraged her to practice her newfound method for at least 40 days. I reminded her that one-ness would always be there for her if and when she desired to return to a mantra practice. She smiled and breathed a sigh of relief that all options were open to her. All options are always open to us, though our constricted, ego-based view of the world sometimes doesn't reveal them to us. But with fear released and a bit of encouragement to expand her comfort zone, my student dove more deeply into her meditation practice, became a teacher of both practices, and now shares both Vipassana and Primordial Sound Meditation with the world. And to this day, I celebrate the amazing wisdom of David Simon and the powerful teaching of Primordial Sound Meditation for helping me to unify the witness inside (the observer), my witnessing (the process of observation), and what I witness (the observed). When that one-ness occurs, everything in my life fuses together in total alignment, and my spiritual practice soars. Rishi devata chandas are all one. Pure unbounded consciousness.

There are more than 1,500 Chopra Center–certified instructors on six continents in more than 500 cities around the world. If you are interested in learning Primordial Sound Meditation, visit **davidji.com**, where you can find a certified meditation teacher in your area, or you can join me through Skype session instruction or at one of my upcoming meditation workshops.

Mantras in Religion

All the world's major religions include some form of mantra meditation in their practices. Chanting the Catholic rosary, practicing Kabalistic hitbodedut meditation, praying one of the Buddhist Lam Rims, repeating Allah's name in Islamic dhikr, or the responsive reading of the Yoga Vasistha: All are repetitive devotional practices giving glory to the divine.

Although meditation in itself is not a religious practice, I find the daily practice of drifting into stillness using a mantra brings me closer to my most universal Self. Thousands of my students who are religious—some of them Orthodox Jews, fundamentalist Christians, and devout Muslims—have found that meditating with a mantra has helped them quiet their minds so they can feel even closer to their God.

Regardless of your religious orientation, when it comes to living a meditation practice, you have to go with what resonates with you, with what feels comfortable, is aligned with your engrained belief systems, works in your home, and feels right to practice on a daily basis. So feel free to choose a mantra that you will be comfortable with and one that supports whatever spiritual or religious philosophies you have as well. Mantra meditation is a beautiful practice that will complement any other religious rituals or spiritual practices you employ.

Whether or not you are religious, you know that there is something bigger—something higher, grander than you—even if it's no more than a belief in a godlike intelligence or creative, universal energy. If you were brought up practicing a religion, you probably still have some devotional aspect to your life. Wherever your belief is directed, I believe that a meditation practice can enhance and uplift your personal devotion to your god of choice, power your prayer, and reaffirm your belief in the divine aspects of life outside of you and within you.

Meditation is simply a tool to help you connect more fully with your most expansive self—the better to feel God or the Universe's love, open yourself to it, and then pour it back into the world. Life is circulation. When the circulation ceases, life ends. When the circulation is total and expansive, you can experience a blissful existence . . . in whatever area of your life that is open to that expansion.

What's the difference between prayer and meditation? Prayer is talking to God; meditation is listening. Meditation does not take the place of prayer in your life. If you have a prayer or devotional practice, your meditation will expand it and make it more powerful. Meditation slows the swirl around you, so you hear the most subtle whispers of God. Meditation heightens your spiritual connection to your higher power, your god, the universe, and your most universal Self.

The Universal Mantra

When David Simon was first diagnosed with a malignant brain tumor in June of 2010, he began incorporating the repetition of what he referred to as "the universal mantra" into his daily practice. In Judaism, it is not appropriate to utter the name of the Lord out loud, so other words are substituted to reference the almighty. The most common of these "no-names" is spelled using four Hebrew letters:

Read left to right, these four consonants YHVH would appear to spell out *Yahweh,* or *Yehovah.* The original Hebrew used no vowels and is read right to left, so it would be spelled from right to left,

The English translation of Yahweh and Yehovah—this personal no-name of the supreme being—is "I am," or "I am that I am." When it is spelled from top to bottom, it appears:

As you can see, it looks like a person with a head, shoulders, arms, and torso, with hips and legs that extend down to the earth.

When you repeat a word or phrase over and over again, it becomes part of your physiology—one with your essence—an integrated aspect of who you are.

To practice what I now refer to as the David Simon Universal Mantra meditation, close your eyes and silently repeat *Yud, Hey, Vov, Hey* over and over. When you notice that you have drifted away from the mantra to thoughts in your mind, sounds in the environment, or sensations in your physical body, gently drift back to Yud, Hey, Vov, Hey. It will get louder and fainter, faster and slower; it will even become jumbled, distorted, and inaudible. However the mantra changes, simply keep repeating it, and when you notice you've drifted away, just gently drift back. Back and forth. Let's try it for a few moments right now. Just for a few moments. But first take a deep breath in through your nostrils, hold it for a moment, and then slowly let it out. Do it again. Then close your eyes, and begin silently repeating the mantra. Let's meditate. How did that feel? What did you feel?

David Simon's universal mantra practice took the one-ness of God into the one-ness of himself until there was no differentiation between the two one-nesses. Pure fusion. Pure merging. Pure universal one-ness. He shared this beautiful practice with the world in the summer of 2010. Pure present-moment awareness—having fully reflected his entire life, absorbed it, and transmuted it into a meditation. He was as close to God as I've ever seen. He was fully established in **BEing**. This inspired me to write the following Sanskrit sutra:

> *Yogastha kareem karuna.*
> *Yogastha kuru karmani.*
> *Yogastha karuna brahma.*

Established in **BEing**, it is a blessing to perform compassionate action. Established in **BEing**, perform action. Established in **BEing**, performing compassionate action is the Ultimate truth.

The phrase "yogastha kuru karmani" is from Chapter 2, Verse 48, in the Bhagavad Gita, in which Lord Krishna counsels the great warrior Arjuna on the purpose of life. Arjuna is deep in the midst of a profound spiritual dilemma, as he knows his purpose in life is to be a fierce warrior, but he is agonized by fear, grief, uncertainty, sadness, and regret as he readies his troops into a calamitous battle in a huge family feud, pitting friend against friend, cousin against cousin, teacher against student, and patriarch against son. As he stands with Krishna, as his charioteer, in the middle of the vast plains of Kurukshetra in northern India, Arjuna gazes intently at the two opposing armies of his relatives that now face each other poised for battle. He is paralyzed by the gravity of the task before him—leading the charge of one army against the other and, in the process, causing the death of hundreds of his friends, esteemed teachers, and relatives. He asks his divine guide how he can possibly live with his decision, and Krishna replies with a spiritual dialogue spanning 18 chapters on yoga, self-realization, dharma (or purpose), devotion to God, the meaning of life, and ultimately, the nature of reality.

The Bhagavad Gita's 700 verses flow like a poetry book of timeless mantras. To meditate on the teachings, select a phrase, such as Chapter 2, Verse 48—"yogastha kuru karmani" (pronounced "yoga-stah koo-roo karmani"; rhymes with Armani) then close your eyes, and silently repeat the phrase over and over as the object of your attention. When you notice that you've drifted away to thoughts, sounds, or physical sensations, gently drift back to "yogastha kuru karmani."

Let's try it right now for a few minutes. Start by saying it out loud three times: yogastha kuru karmani, yogastha kuru karmani, yogastha kuru karmani. Then whisper it three times: yogastha kuru karmani, yogastha kuru karmani, yogastha kuru karmani. Now repeat it silently to yourself three times: yogastha kuru karmani, yogastha kuru karmani, yogastha kuru karmani. Then silently repeat it over and over. Take a deep breath in and slowly exhale. Now close your eyes and say the mantra. I'll wait right here.

Did you notice that your attention flowed to and from the mantra, disconnecting for a moment here and there from your awareness of thoughts, sounds, and physical sensations? Did you notice yourself drift back and forth? What did you feel? How did it feel?

Mantra Myths

Many spiritual teachers assert that there is a specific protocol to rigidly observe regarding mantras—that they need to be taught in a certain way, used in a certain way, used only at certain times. This makes sense to a point, so you can understand the basic structure and process of a mantra meditation and get grounded in it. But I have observed that when the practice starts to take on a rigid atmosphere of "musts" and "rules," personal commitment and passion seem to ebb. Meditation and the desire to do it must flow naturally from who we have become and must feel like something we *want* to do, not something we feel we *must* do. Infinite flexibility is the key to happiness and fulfillment. This applies to use of the mantra as well.

There is so much conversation about mantras in the meditation community that I wanted to share my thoughts on the most popular assumptions and misconceptions regarding mantra practice and demystify some of it.

1. The mantra must be pronounced perfectly.

Everything in our world is about attention and intention. If your intention is to connect to the subtle essence of the vibration, don't be critical of yourself regarding the pronunciation or the esoteric meaning of the mantra you're using. While some claim that a mispronounced mantra will be ineffective, if your intention is pure, the mantra will resonate and have purpose, even if you are pronouncing it differently from how it was originally uttered. There are many Sanskrit dictionaries and pronunciation websites online, so feel free to explore the many expressions of Sanskrit.

2. Mantras are to be taken very seriously.

Many of the mantras we use so casually today had their beginnings in devotional or religious contexts. While we may use the name of various gods as metaphors—such as awakening your

Christ consciousness, opening your heart to your true Buddha nature, or enlisting Ganesh to help you solve problems—when invoking mantras with deities, one should have sensitivity to the thousands of years of practice and devotion that have preceded this moment and the depth of sacredness that should be acknowledged and respected. All mantras (meaningful and meaningless) should be treated with reverence, essentially *handled with care* in a lighthearted, innocent, and gentle way. They should be treated not with the seriousness of someone about to perform a science experiment or a medical operation but as someone appreciating the effectiveness of the tool.

That being said, too much seriousness or importance on the mantra brings you into the realm of meaning, of thought, of activity. That's why the silent repetition of the mantra will always take you deeper than the out loud repetition: one is passive . . . the other has many moving parts, such as your breath, your voice, its tone, its timbre, its volume, and the sound itself as it leaves your lips, travels through air into your ears, and vibrates your chest, creating another entire loop of activity. The lighter the practice, the easier the practice. The easier the practice, the more likelihood that you will continue the practice. The more consistent you can be with the practice, the more quickly you will see and feel changes within you and outside of you. So lighten up!

3. To be most effective, a mantra should be received directly from a self-realized teacher so that it's infused with the teacher's spiritual energy.

All forms of interaction carry an energetic exchange—smiling at someone, having a conversation, kissing, shaking hands, making a transaction, honking your car horn, making love, even reading this book, and, of course, receiving your mantra from a teacher. But it must be kept in perspective; a mantra is just a tool. And a great teacher can help you to use that tool by egolessly channeling the knowledge of the universe and open you to wisdom that already rests within you. It's important to remember that once information has been transmitted to you, the true teacher holds no further claim on the information or what you do with it.

Receiving your mantra directly from a teacher is ideal, because you can continue to work with the teacher as your practice evolves. But the teacher is simply a conduit for you to open to the practice, receive your mantra, refine your technique, and evolve in its ongoing use. Some teachers carry a higher vibration. Some have greater depth. Some are better facilitators of your learning process. Some are more personable. Some are better communicators. Some have a teaching style that may resonate more with you. Some have more consistent practices of their own. It's important to consider all these factors when choosing a teacher, but regardless of the energy or state of consciousness of your teacher, *you* are the only one who can give value to the mantra in your life. That happens only through daily practice. So right now, with the support of this book, you will be able to comfortably meditate. So don't stress about the power of the teacher; believe in the power of your practice . . . the power of *you*. Use the tools, and see where your life goes.

4. To keep the power of the mantra at a high level, it should be kept in strictest secrecy and not revealed to anyone else.

The mantra is your mind vehicle that takes you from activity to stillness and silence. You wouldn't use sound to take you into silence, so what keeps the mantra powerful is keeping it in a sacred place and not using it casually or out loud, even when you're by yourself. If I gave you a seed for a magnificent flower, you planted it, and then months later I bumped into you and asked how your seed was growing, you wouldn't dig into the earth and show me your seed. You'd say, "I planted it, and it's blooming . . . it's blossoming." We do the same with our mantras. We keep them planted in the stillness and the silence to be used as our mind vehicle in the sacred fertile soil of our practice.

Bringing your mantra from the ether into this physical world by sharing it with others will also lead to you applying some kind of meaning to it, defeating the purpose of a *meaningless* vibration.

Of course, sharing your mantra with someone won't trigger some cosmic retribution upon your karma. Yet you can't unring the bell. You can't take it back. So if you'd like your mantra to have its optimal effectiveness, it starts with not sharing it and keeping it in the realm of meaninglessness. If someone is asking, do they really care? Or are they simply being polite? I recommend that you keep it private until you are very comfortable with it being planted firmly within. I prefer to keep mine private and meaningless so that it most effectively disconnects me from meaning and activity.

To keep your mantra sacred, when you find yourself repeating it or using it when doing some activity other than meditation, just let your awareness drift back to your thoughts in the same way that you drift from thought to the mantra during meditation. Deep attachment to the mantra as a word or incantation will move you deeper into meaning and into activity. Remember that we use the mantra to disconnect us from activity, so don't spend time on its meaning or definition. Use it for its timeless, meaningless, effortless, vibrational power.

5. YOUR MANTRA CAN HELP YOU FALL BACK TO SLEEP.

If you're having trouble sleeping, don't use a mantra you use in meditation to help you fall back asleep. You don't want to reinforce a Pavlovian connection between saying your mantra and falling asleep. Deepak taught me a sleep-inducing mantra called the sleep mantra. The mantra is *Om Agasthi Shaheena* (pronounced "om ah-gahs-tee sha-hee-na"). Although it works whether you repeat it silently or out loud, my recommendation is to start by saying it out loud three times, soften to a whisper, and then move it into silence. Established in BEing, perform action.

Mantra meditations can help you transcend.

CHAPTER ELEVEN

Secrets of
Chanting Meditation

*"Some scenes you juggle two balls, some scenes you
juggle three balls, some scenes you can juggle five balls.
The key is always to speak in your own voice.
Speak the truth."*

— Vincent D'Onofrio

The sun was just beginning to peek its head up as I was gliding down the Mekong River in northern Cambodia. The thick balmy air was penetrated by the occasional voices of monks performing their first prayers of the day. As the morning slowly unfolded and we silently drifted downstream, the chanting became more frequent. As we winded our way down the river, one voice ahead would coax us in, fill the air as we approached, fill our ears as we passed by, and then trail off as we moved on to the next new voice ahead of us, which would beckon us again, fill the air, and fade into the distance as we continued our morning glide downstream.

This gauntlet of Theravada Buddhist prayer created an ongoing vibrational blanketing of my senses as one monk's voice faded out and an approaching one faded in. And on and on the chanting continued for miles as we silently followed the current downstream. With my eyes closed, I sat at the bow of the boat, drinking in the singsong of prayer until it actually became me. The repetition of Buddha's teachings in the ancient Pali language surrounded me and rippled through me for over an hour. As we passed the last temple and the final monk's prayer vanished into the mist like the subtle waning vibrations of a gong slowing into stillness, tears streamed from my eyes at the simple beauty of one-ness. Surrendering to the rising and falling waves of devotion, in a language I did not even understand, connected me deeply to some sweet core of my being and disconnected me for those few hours from any mental activity, such as thoughts of the past or the future. In surrendering to the chanting, I had ultimately become the vibration and had absorbed its devotional intentions even though I could not decipher the words. It was a profound meditation.

To this day, in addition to my daily Primordial Sound Meditation practice, I enjoy chanting mantras out loud to bring me to higher states of consciousness. My favorite five that I encourage you to Google or find on YouTube are the Gayatri Mantra, so devotionally chanted by Deva Premal; the shanti mantra, a part of my daily ritual since 2003 and sung by all Primordial Sound Meditation instructors around the world when they teach a student his or her primordial sound mantra; the hanuman chalisa, first sung to me by the sage Bhagavan Das, with the empowering encouragement in its final verse: *Pavantnai sankat haran, Mangal murti roop,* translated as, "Oh! Conqueror of the Wind, Destroyer of all miseries, you are a symbol of Auspiciousness"; the sri durga aarti, celebrating the divine fusion of compassion and power in a spiritual warrior and the awakening of our divine feminine Shakti energy; and the *Mahamrityunjaya Mantra* also called the *Tryambakam Mantra,* known as the death-defying mantra. It is chanted to restore health and vitality to those in weakened states and is pronounced:

Aum tryambakam yajāmahe
Sugandhim pusti-vardhanam
Urvārukam iva bandhanān
Mrtyor muksīya māmrtāt

The practice of chanting performs many of the same functions and benefits as a silent meditation but instead of being in stillness, the chanter achieves a state of physical/emotional trance through the process of continuously repeating a sound, word, mantra, or the name of God, as in the example of David Simon's Universal Mantra.

Devotional chanting goes back thousands of years and has been celebrated in ritual and religion as a way to achieve deeper contact with the divine by shifting attention from the past or future to the present moment. The premise is that during this process, your attention can only be on the sounds you utter or hear— not on any other thought, sound, or sensation. This is exactly what I experienced that morning cruising down the Mekong River in Cambodia. The continuous repetition of words, mantras, vibrations, or sutras—whether in the form of prayer, song, or responsive reading—creates a state of higher consciousness, but the delivery system is one of the physical and mental realms.

When you utter sounds, you are using the tools of your voice (your mouth, your tongue, your vocal cords, uvula, throat, lungs, and your breath), and the effect is for the outer ear, known as the *pinna* (the part that extends from your head to capture sound waves and direct them down into your external ear canal). These mechanical sound waves bump against the tympanic membrane (your ear drum) and make it vibrate. When your eardrum vibrates, it tickles the first of three ossicles (the three smallest bones in your body!) sending the vibration along in a very specific sequence.

The first ossicle called the malleus (because it is mallet shaped) vibrates against your second ossicle called the incus (because it is anvil shaped), which then vibrates against your third ossicle known as the stapes (because it is stirrup shaped). The stapes then vibrates against the window of the cochlea (meaning snail-shaped structure), which is filled with fluid. The vibration creates a pressure wave in this cochlear fluid that then travels deep inside the cochlea into the organ of Corti, which has tiny hairs suspended in the fluid and sends signals toward the brain. At this point, the mechanical energy becomes a neural signal that we understand as sound. It is then that the intellect, and then the soul, resonates with the sounds.

The reason drifting down the river that morning was so powerful for me was that I was in a passive state, one of innocence and receptivity. I wasn't chanting, moving my lips, opening or closing my mouth, or pushing air with any force. I was simply absorbing and vibrating. It was more like experiencing a glorious *Gandharva* massage treatment. In the Buddhist traditions, chanting the *Buddhavacana* (considered the direct guidance of the Buddha) is a powerful way of effortlessly etching the teachings of Buddhism into one's being. They were etched into my being that morning on the river as wave after wave of the Buddhavacana rippled through my body.

Buddhist chanting is not practiced so much as ritual but rather as a way to develop mindfulness—keeping the mind in the present. The Buddhist meditation practitioner does not worship the Buddha or ask for forgiveness or blessings. Instead, the practitioner honors the divine teachings and respects the Buddha for his supreme achievement.

As most early Buddhist texts were written in the language of Pali, much Buddhist chanting stays true to that lineage, while Hindu chanting is in Sanskrit. The teachings of these two belief systems have been interwoven for thousands of years, and transmitting these texts orally has been the most organic method of keeping the teachings alive and growing throughout generations.

Whether uttered in Pali or Sanskrit, this measured, monotonous song or prayer is repeated over and over to create a trance-like, vibrational state that moves the chanter and the listener from meaning to meaninglessness, and from a state of egoistic individuality to one of expanded awareness or universality. At the same time, through ritualized repetition, the teachings get woven into every fiber of the chanter's and the listener's being.

Japa

When the chanter brings the chanting down to a whisper and repeats the same prayer or phrasing over and over, this whispered repetition is known as *japa*, which in Sanskrit means "muttering" or "whispering." Most japa is accompanied by a ritual in which the chanter counts the number of repetitions of the mantra on a *mala*, a prayer bracelet or necklace made of 108 beads. Usually held in the right hand during japa practice, the mala is often draped over the middle finger so that you can flick one bead and then the next with your thumb as you repeat the mantra over and over. In Eastern traditions, the index finger is said to represent the ego, which is seen as the biggest obstacle to experiencing self-realization.

Therefore, in japa practice, we don't touch the mala to the index finger. After you have rolled 108 beads over with your thumb, you arrive at a larger bead known as the *meru* or "guru bead" or "head of Shiva," which signals you to stop and flick the beads in the opposite direction. This way you can track how many repetitions you've done without opening your eyes or keeping track in your mind by counting. The practice of japa is thousands of years old, beginning as the personal expressions of the thousands of verses in the sacred Rig Veda, Hinduism's oldest and holiest scripture, which was shared solely in oral form for 2,000 years before being written down around 1,500 years ago. Over time, the mantras used in japa evolved from non-Vedic sources as well, such as the Hindu Tantric texts or those cognized by meditating rishis.

Bhajan, Kirtan, and Namavali

Any Indian devotional song is referred to as *bhajan* (which comes from the Sanskrit term *bhakti,* meaning "devotion"). While japa is always meant to be whispered or chanted to one's self, when the words or mantras are sung rather than whispered, that is considered bhajan.

When the group becomes larger and there is a leader, this group chanting is known as *kirtan,* meaning "to repeat" in Sanskrit. The person conducting the kirtan—the *kirtanker*—leads the group in call-and-response Sanskrit chanting. Kirtan practice involves chanting hymns or mantras to the accompaniment of instruments such as the harmonium (a hybrid instrument that is like a cross between a mini lap piano and an accordion), the two-headed mrdanga, a pakawaj drum, or karatal hand cymbals. Kirtan was first popularized as a part of Vaishnava worship (a form of worship of the Hindu god Lord Vishnu—the maintainer of the Universe),

Sikhism, and specific Buddhist traditions. In recent years, however, kirtan has also become a frequent feature of the yoga and meditation communities perched at the door of the mainstream market. Paramahansa Yogananda (philosopher, guru, author of *Autobiography of a Yogi,* and creator of the Self-Realization Fellowship) was one of the first Eastern spiritual teachers to bring kirtan to the West. In 1923, he led a kirtan with 3,000 people at New York City's Carnegie Hall, chanting Guru Nanak's "Hey Hari Sundara" ("Oh God Beautiful"). That's right . . . Carnegie Hall!

Kirtan is currently becoming more widely known in the West, with the increased popularity and celebrity of skilled kirtankers and practitioners of *namavali*—songs that worship Hindu deities such as Lord Rama or Lord Krishna with devotional anecdotes or by recounting episodes from scriptures or verses that chronicle the multiple names of God. Modern masters of these meditative practices, such as Snatam Kaur, Guru Ganesha, Deva Premal, Jai Utal, and Miten, have expanded on the groundbreaking, multi-decade careers of master kirtankers Krishna Das and Bhagavan Das. New, edgy, up-and-coming kirtankers include MC Yogi, who blends kirtan with rap; Larisa Stow, who mixes devotional music with motivational interludes; and Grammy-nominated singer-songwriter Beth Neilson Chapman, who expanded her creative success in the pop and country markets and took the realm of Sanskrit chanting by storm in 2011 by recording classic chants selected by David Simon. All of these talented musicians are attracting crossover audiences with their more diverse and eclectic styles.

An easy way to learn about chanting is by listening to chants online or downloading them to your iPod, tablet, or phone and playing them as background music to your day. The chanting recordings of those I've just mentioned are amazing ways to experience the timeless chanting of mantras in very different styles and a great foundation to exploring the realm of kirtan and namavali. They all have CDs, YouTube videos, and downloads available online.

Chanting meditations can help you express yourself.

PART III

FURTHER ALONG THE PATH

By now, you understand the history, art, and science of meditation; its powerful, clinically proven benefits; and the most popular ancient and modern techniques. We've meditated together and perhaps even spent some time in the gap together. I've crafted this section as your daily practice resource guide to help you get started, share some powerful nuances, and fill in some of the answers you may seek as your practice evolves. Let's begin by discussing what's supposed to happen when you meditate, so we can demystify this somewhat secretive stigma surrounding the experience.

CHAPTER TWELVE

EXPERIENCES IN MEDITATION

"Do you have patience to wait until your mud settles and the water is clear? Can you remain unmoving until the right action arises by itself?"

— LAO-TZU

Only a few things can happen when you meditate. And they are all valid experiences. No matter what method you are using as the object of your attention (mantra, visual, breath, chanting, chakra . . .), there are only three things that can actually happen when you meditate *in addition* to the object of your attention:

You can *have thoughts.*
You can *fall asleep.* You can *experience stillness.*

This stillness is referred to as "the gap," an expression often attributed to Maharishi Mahesh Yogi, the great sage and founder of the Transcendental Meditation movement, yet used by millions worldwide to describe the experience of pure consciousness during meditation. Self-development author and motivational speaker Dr. Wayne Dyer has referred to the gap as the place where we "join forces with our sacred energy and regain the power of our Source (God)."

I define the gap as a place of no space and no time. No space means you can't know you're there; no time means you can't know for how long. Yet everyone is trying to get there!

Nine months following the 9/11 attack on the Twin Towers of the World Trade Center, I was meditating with Deepak in the historic city of Oxford, England. It was the day of the week that they mow all the lawns within the grounds of the university, which stretches for miles throughout the historic city. Giant green mowing machines 25-feet wide and looking like oversized, winged, mechanical predators from a science-fiction movie, buzzed the thousands of acres of grass surrounding the thick stone walls of our medieval-era room. The sound was deafening. Even though the room temperature was a sweltering 90 degrees, I got up to close the Harry Potter–like sliver windows of the room to block out the noise of the swarming mowers. As I got up, Deepak asked me where I was going.

When I responded that I was trying to block out the noise so it wouldn't distract me during the meditation, he smiled and said, "There's no difference between the sound of those mowers, a beautiful love song, a baby crying, the sound of your mantra, or even me whispering in your ear. They are all simply thoughts, and when you notice that you have left the mantra and drifted into any thought, any sound, or any sensation, just gently drift back to the mantra." I sat back down.

Those words have stuck with me since that moment, and often when I realize in my meditation that I have been making mental lists or thinking about a conversation I had or a challenge that is before me—on realizing that I have drifted away from the mantra to thoughts, sounds, or physical sensations—I simply return my attention to the mantra. It's important to underscore that the three activities of the mind and the physical realm—thoughts, sounds, and physical sensations—are actually all versions of having thoughts. But to understand the process of going beyond them, let's first explore them.

Thoughts During Meditation

As I have mentioned previously, we have between 60,000 and 80,000 thoughts a day; that's a thought about every one to one-and-a-half seconds. But you are *not* your thoughts. You are the space between each thought. And in this space of infinite possibilities lies the pure potentiality of the next thought. Most people think they are their thoughts, but we simply receive our thoughts. Like a cell phone, you receive transmissions aimed at you; you don't receive other people's calls, texts, or e-mails. There are literally thousands of texts, e-mails, and phone calls flying all around us in each moment, but only the ones meant for our phone number or e-mail address land on us. Just as you wouldn't say your cell phone *is* your texts, e-mails, or phone calls, the *you* that rests beneath all these layers is not your thoughts. You have thoughts, but you are not thoughts.

Your cell phone is not your texts. Your cell phone receives texts and then they fill your phone's memory. But the phone is not texts just because it has received them. That's the same thing as you and your thoughts. You have them. They pour into you; some get stored, and some get deleted. Some blow right by. But you are not your thoughts. You are the stillness and silence—the pure potentiality that rests beneath all these layers of thought.

Thoughts have two characteristics: they are silent, and they have meaning. So throughout our lives, as thoughts drift in, we build a foundation of meaning and then we continue to build more and more meaning around that thought and then build that even larger or move to another thought. That next thought is birthed from all your experiences, coupled with infinite possibilities of pure potentiality. That's why the next thought can be anything. And no matter what that next thought is, *it still is not you*. It is simply another thought—regardless of how profound it may seem.

So it is normal to have thoughts . . . thoughts of boredom . . . thoughts of restlessness . . . thoughts of saying to yourself, "It's not working," or "How could it work? I'm not doing it right," or "I'm thinking about my love life" (or "my job" or "a conversation"), or "How long has it been?" This is normal, and when you first become aware during meditation, it's simply your conditioned bodymind letting you know that it's not used to stillness. It's sending you messages of resistance to the stillness. Be gentle. And stay the course. With each meditation, you will become more comfortable with the gentle drift back and forth between activity and stillness.

So our thoughts are constructions and constrictions that keep us in activity, trying to make sense of every moment in some way. But we are not our thoughts. Which means, in any moment, we can drift from them back to the present . . . in which there is no thought . . . there is no sound . . . there is no fear . . . there is no constriction or loss or grief or sadness . . . only light . . . pure unbounded consciousness . . . pure perfection. There is only this precious moment.

We can disconnect from thought very easily in meditation by drifting back to the object of our attention, such as our breath or the mantra.

Sounds During Meditation

Sound is a powerful creator of thought and a subcategory of thought. As long as we are gifted with functional eardrums, we will hear sound. We can close our eyelids to stop seeing, but we don't have a biological mechanism to stop sound. And because none of us lives in a soundproof booth or a recording studio, we will hear sound in our daily life and as part of our daily meditation.

Dogs bark, airplanes fly overhead, car alarms go off, and phones ring. Welcome to Planet Earth! Meditation takes you beyond sound, so don't feel the need to do anything with it. Let it in. Witness it. Observe its flow into your awareness . . . hang with it a bit if you care to . . . and then observe it flow away as your attention drifts back to the mantra, your breath, or the object of your attention. Remember: Do nothing with it. You are the one who gives the sound relevance, so at first you will want to listen and have an internal dialogue about it, which will most likely create thought and then more dialogue. When you notice you are having an internal conversation about a sound, ever so gently drift back to the mantra, or your breath, or whatever the object of your attention is during the meditation.

Just like your thoughts, sounds are not interruptions in your meditation; they are part of the fabric of your meditation. They *are* your meditation. Don't feel the need to do anything with sound; simply let it vibrate, and gently drift back to the mantra, your breath, or the object of your attention. Ultimately, the mantra or the inhale and exhale of your breathing can be the loudest sound in your awareness. As Deepak reminded me a decade ago, "There is no difference between a beautiful love song or a baby crying." It's the intention we bring to the sound that determines its relevance in the moment. The longer you stay on a particular sound, the closer it leads you to some kind of meaning and then to thought. Whether it's a samba and you feel like dancing, a crow relentlessly chanting its shrill bark over and over again, or even the faint hum of the next-door neighbor's TV, the longer you linger, the more thoughts will converge to develop a story. Then a parade of thoughts will begin as you play out a dialogue. It is our desire for—and our connection to—*meaning* that sparks all thought. So do nothing with sound. Let it come; let it go; be unconcerned.

Easier said than done given that we are in this flesh casing that contains ears, which contain eardrums, three tiny bones that vibrate uncontrollably, and a liquid inner ear filled with microscopic hairs that connect to the eighth cranial nerve, which sends detailed messages from the cochlea to the brain on feeling sound waves. But again, all this happens without your direction, intellectual analysis, or personal input. So in meditation, your awareness that there is another vibration—this one with no meaning—that you can drift back to allows you to gently disconnect from whatever the sound is that is vibrating your physiology.

Try to listen to two conversations simultaneously. You can't really do it. Try it with your TV or radio. Ask someone to engage you in conversation while you are deeply engrossed in a show that contains dialogue. You can really only follow one series of vibrations. You may drift back and forth, quickly grabbing a word here or there from both conversations, and your eardrum is vibrating to accommodate all frequencies being transmitted to it. But at the level of the intellect, you are in overload and can't actually process them both simultaneously. Now envision that the ongoing conversation in your head is the ongoing repetition of a mantra. As long as you are always willing to drift back to it, the mantra will disconnect you from thoughts and especially sounds.

Another example of attention and intention regarding sound is happening right now as you read this book. There may be many sounds in the background, but as long as your attention is on the words on these pages and your intention is to keep reading, the outside sounds drift in and out and don't take you away from the flow of information. But if you weren't resonating with a particular sentence or paragraph, you are more susceptible to being interrupted by a sound. Remember . . . the mantra can always be the loudest, most primary vibration in your awareness.

THE POWER OF INTENTION

It's the intention we have about objects and experiences that defines them in our life. That's why some of us love dogs and some of us are afraid of them. Some of us love Metallica, while others resonate with Barry Manilow. Some of us lean left, and others stand on the right. Some of us love pasta and others crave gluten-free offerings. But that's simply the intention *we* bring to a given situation. It's not those things that are inherently good or bad or right or wrong; it is the intention each of us brings to a particular object or experience.

See how so many beliefs and affinities in your life would shift if just a few of the things you rejected, detested, feared, and repressed suddenly were on your "like" list. Everything would be different. Each day unravel something you reject—just one thing—and embrace it just for the day. Show compassion for someone you are mad at; smile at something that usually makes you grimace or groan; instead of rolling your eyes, offer help. Use the mantra *san kalpa* (pronounced "san kalp"), which means "subtle intention." Simply by being aware of your intention, it will grow from the shadows into the light. Try this meditation exercise for a week, and you will feel a powerful shift.

Sensations During Meditation

Another generator of thought is our physical body. Physical sensations are a fact of life. We have this flesh casing, which in Sanskrit is called the *annamaya kosha,* the "sheath covering made up of food." We are indeed DNA wrapped in food. As long as we have the blessing of a physical body, we will experience sensation. We will wring our hands, furrow our brow, feel gurgles in our stomach, rise and fall with each breath, and scratch the proverbial itch. Don't let the fact that you have a physical existence frustrate or upset you. Celebrate that your flesh vehicle has moved you through life up to this moment.

When it comes to your body, always move toward comfort. If you have anxiety about how long you've been meditating, open your eyes and look at the clock or your watch. If your legs have gotten numb from sitting, uncross them. If your head has slouched down, gently lift it back to a more comfortable position. If that doesn't work, find a blanket or pillow to support your neck. Find a chair where you can be comfortable. Yes, it's okay if it reclines a bit. You don't want to lie down or re-create a sleeping position, but pretty much any chair you feel comfortable in will work.

When I'm meditating while sitting in a chair, I don't cross one leg over, resting my ankle on my other knee, because I know that my ankle gets pins and needles in about 14 minutes. At the 14-minute mark, my attention flows to my numb ankle, and *boom,* I'm back here in the local domain in the realm of activity as I uncross and stretch my legs. Get yourself as comfortable as possible, so your physical body is not a factor during the meditation.

As for timing your meditation, feel free to face the direction of a clock, watch, or timer. I place a clock right in front of my gaze so that if I should open my eyes a crack, I'll see the time in less than a second, and I can seamlessly drift back into my meditation. I prefer that to waiting for an alarm, but it's a matter of preference. And if you'd prefer to be signaled at the 30-minute point or a specific interval, every cell phone on the planet has an alarm, and most phones have ringtones and apps that mimic chiming Tibetan bowls or similar soothing sounds to gently take you out of the meditation. Ideally, choose a soft sound that gets progressively louder. Visit **davidji.com** to download free meditation timers that range from 5 minutes to 45 minutes.

When I sit in a chair to meditate, I like to have my feet touch the ground. If there is no chair, or if I am home, I can sit comfortably on a fat (six inches high) zafu pillow with my legs crossed for about an hour before I need to readjust. Since you are only meditating for 30 minutes at a time, your goal should be to find some seating arrangement that will feel comfortable for at least that period.

If your back hurts, stop and rub it a bit, or stand up and stretch it. But then go back to finish meditating for the remaining minutes of your practice. Honor your body with any need that you have. Then gently reimmerse yourself into your practice by taking a few deep breaths and then floating back into your mantra.

If you have engaged in strenuous physical activity, allow yourself a cooldown before leaping into meditation. So wait a bit after yoga or exercise to let your racing heart settle down. You don't want to enter the practice hyperventilating.

You also don't want to bring any alternative medicines—such as caffeine, cannabis, or alcohol—into your meditation. Wait until after you've meditated before you choose whether to ingest one of those recreational additives. Why? They will get in the way of authentic experiences. They will make it more challenging for you to genuinely "feel" the beauty of the actual meditation and, most likely, the post-meditation follow-through of your unconditioned self. There's plenty of time throughout the rest of your day to bring in one or more of these "healing" supplements. I enjoy wine and the occasional margarita. Yet, I find that when I am meditating a lot, I have no desire to drink. In fact, it's the last thing on my mind during the Seduction of Spirit meditation retreats. I just want to hang in that higher state of consciousness forever, and I have noticed that any "additive" dulls the clarity and benefits of my meditation practice.

As long as we are alive, we will feel. We are pure, unbounded consciousness wrapped in this flesh casing of tender molecules for the span of a lifetime, and as many have observed, "No one gets out of here alive." Accept the fact that as long as you are living, sensations will always be a part of life and, therefore, a part of meditation.

How Do I Know If It's Working?

Thinking, hearing, and feeling are the only three activities that we engage during meditation, but there are only three experiences you could genuinely have during the meditation. In addition to the object of attention (repeating a mantra, following your breath, or chanting some no-name of the divine), you can (1) fall asleep, (2) have thoughts, and (3) drift into stillness and silence known as being in the gap. *All are signs of a verified meditation.* If any, all, or a combination occur during your practice, that is the sign of a verified meditation.

Every other experience (worry, regret, expectation, hearing, visuals, sensations) is a version of a thought. We'll now discuss a few more common experiences.

Common Beginner Experiences

New meditators often comment that they feel a sensation in their head. Some cite an overall peace of mind or a calming feeling that, over time, continues to weave through all aspects of their life. Other new meditators cite boredom and restlessness. This is very common and is to be expected. We spend every single moment of our life in activity. To suddenly stop that activity addiction or do nothing . . . *really* do nothing . . . is an interruption to the person who has been trying to fill those empty spaces with TV, books, painkillers, magazines, music, alcohol, sleep, drugs, sex, crossword puzzles, slot machines, and Web surfing. A small group of new meditators report either a slight dizziness, a tightness in their scalp, throbbing temples, or an outright headache. If this happens to you, it usually means you are working too hard. Take a few more deep breaths before and during meditation. This will allow you to release a bit of stress before you drift into stillness. And don't work so hard on perfecting your practice; don't do anything. Let go, and the tightness in your head will fade away.

Still others report a gentle tingling around the location of the third eye. Throughout time, this energy center has been linked to one's connection to source, to a spiritual practice, to intuition, to spirit itself. This is a common place to have feeling during meditation. If you feel sensation in your third eye, simply see it as an energetic connection between you and your soul. But remember, it's still just a thought, so try not to place too much meaning on it.

RELEASING STRESS

One of the first things that new meditators experience is the release of stress. Over your life, you have built up tension in your belly, your hands, your jaw, your back, your neck, your shoulders, your cheeks—essentially your whole body. And if it's there, it's in your flesh, in your muscles, in your bones . . . in all of your cells . . . in every drop of blood that flows through you, impacting and influencing your emotional and physical health. Meditation helps to release stress, which we can define as all the wishes, dreams, expectations, and desires in which a need you had was not met. How many times a day do you turn an unmet need into an emotional or physical disturbance? How many times a day do you go back to the past to figure out why or how a need was not met? We spend a lot of time in the land of unmet needs, and how we respond to them determines our stress levels. These disturbances weave their vibration into every aspect of our being, and unless we interpret it differently or get closure, it will continue to fester at the most subtle level. This has built up within you over the course of your entire life. But now you have a tool to slowly let these constricted aspects of you slowly ease out of your self.

It is very common for a new meditator to express the release of stress in different ways: some sigh, some smile more, some cry, some feel the release in their body, some feel more grounded, some have flashes of clarity, some have aha! moments, some become more sensitive or more emotional, some have flashes of compassion or empathy where they did not previously, while others have visual experiences. This is you becoming more aware of your unconditioned self.

As you begin to witness these experiences, try not to shut down. A lot of this experience is the "waking up" of your once-dormant, emotionally toxic plaque that has been woven from the threads of every unmet need throughout the course of your life. This emotional release is standing in the way of you and unconditional love, between you and happiness, between you and peace of mind. Remember to be gentle with yourself as the "new" lighter you begins to emerge, and some of your less-nourishing patterns start to drift away. Stress can also release itself through the physical body in the form of lightness or heaviness in the upper body, tingling sensations, cold or hot feelings in the hands or feet, pins and needles, and soft waves of energy flowing through certain parts of your body. In the first two weeks of a new meditation practice, you will have myriad experiences through which you will express the release of stress. Write about these experiences in your journal, not simply what you experience during the meditation but what happens in the other 23 hours of your day—your experiences *outside* of meditation.

VISUAL IMAGES

Some of us are more visual than others. We see the world through images. So during meditation, it would be natural to see geometric shapes, saturations of color, the mantra or other words, symbols, drawings, photographs, or even videos. Many people see the faces of people they have never met as well as the faces of loved ones, or those who have passed on from this earthly realm. When you see colors, it means there is an energetic movement in the chakra of that color. You can refer to Chapter 7, "Secrets of Energy Meditation," to discover the meaning of each color.

FALLING ASLEEP

Your bodymind always gets what it needs when you meditate. Sometimes thoughts pour in so we can process our day; sometimes we experience pure stillness and silence; and sometimes, drifting into sleep is really what we need. If you realize that you've fallen asleep in the middle of your meditation, *"Bravo!"* Obviously, it means that you relaxed enough to surrender to your bodymind's restoration process. Don't scold yourself for falling asleep since that's one of the three experiences that can happen when you meditate—and therefore a powerful sign of a verified meditation. If you always fall asleep, then it means you are not getting enough rest. But the next time you fall asleep in meditation, commend yourself for slowing down rather than scolding yourself for being a loser!

Again, the encouragement here is to simply let it happen, let it flow—the images, the thoughts, the sounds, the sleep, the stress release, the stillness—and within two weeks, you will be operating on an entirely different plane of existence, a higher plane than you were only a few weeks earlier. This will not weaken you; it will not make you a slacker, lazy, or uncaring. It will give you a broader perspective on life. Pay attention not only to what you experience during the meditation but what happens in the other 23 hours of your day. That's where the true magnificence and benefits of meditation begin to flower.

That's where the magic happens and that's where you will see signs of how meditation is benefiting your life. These experiences are teachers in your personal development and evolution. You will be amazed by what you find after only a few days, and that will be the best confirmation of your personal transformation. You will see more; you will understand more. You will love more deeply. You will live more deeply.

CHAPTER THIRTEEN

THE FIVE MYTHS OF MEDITATION

*"What's the message in Metallica? There is no message,
but if there was a message, it really should be look within
yourself, don't listen to me, don't listen to James, don't
listen to anybody, look within yourself for the answers."*

— LARS ULRICH

Most of what we know about meditation, we learned years ago from watching David Carradine in his role as "Grasshopper," or Kwai Chang Caine, on the anachronistic TV show *Kung Fu,* or reading Somerset Maugham's tale of experiencing one-ness in *The Razor's Edge,* or watching Jim Carrey levitating in the jungle with the monkey and the guano in that second *Ace Ventura* movie. Perhaps you saw Oprah, Eckhart Tolle, Louise Hay, Deepak Chopra, Dr. Oz, or Wayne Dyer espousing the benefits of meditation on television, or you read about it in one of their books. Or maybe you dropped into a weekend meditation workshop at a local yoga studio.

Wherever you got your original understanding of the practice of meditation, there are five basic myths that we all come across at some point in our attempts to develop a meditation practice. Embracing these myths helped us to rationalize that our lives would be better off *without* meditation. And ultimately, this rests at the core of why we may have stopped or let it slip away. But if you can embrace these myths as just that—myths—and then release them from your belief system, you will more easily give yourself permission to begin or reengage your practice.

MYTH #1: THE FIRST THING YOU NEED TO DO IS TO CLEAR THE THOUGHTS FROM YOUR MIND OR AT LEAST STILL THEM.

As if!

You have between 60,000 and 80,000 thoughts a day. That's approximately one thought every 1.2 seconds. They're coming. You will not stop them, so don't even try. Don't lift a finger to resist or stop or do anything with your thoughts. They are not interruptions in your meditation; they *are part* of your meditation, so let them come and let them go. Simply drift back to the mantra, or your breath, or whatever else you were using to disconnect you from activity. So many meditators stop meditating because they have thoughts, but having thoughts flowing in and out of your meditation is so perfect. This is your chance to process each day's activities that otherwise would go buried, unaddressed, and unprocessed.

That doesn't mean to pay attention to them . . . and that includes not resisting them either. To resist is to place attention on, and where attention goes, energy flows. Treat thoughts as you would clouds. Let them drift in, and let them drift away. Don't engage them. Simply drift back to the object of your attention—the mantra, your breath, the drishti, and so on. Here's how much effort to use when you meditate: Like mist rising off a lake at dawn.

Stop now, and envision morning mist ever so gently lifting off a field or a lake; there is virtually no movement. That's how hard you should "work" or "try" to meditate. You can't stop thoughts, and you can't clear the mind. So don't even bother. Let the thoughts flow; be unconcerned and drift back to the mantra. Just keep drifting back and forth. Continue to float your attention back to the mantra, and ultimately, over time, you will find that during meditation, you spend more time in mantra land than in thought land; more time in the realm of no-meaning than in the realm of meaning; more time in stillness than in activity. And as you meditate each day, the fluctuations of your mind will slow. The parade of thoughts will slow as each is met by the tiniest bit of stillness . . . of silence.

MYTH #2: SOMETHING SPECIAL OR TRANSCENDENT IS SUPPOSED TO HAPPEN DURING MEDITATION.

Nothing special is supposed to happen during meditation. Blissful, calming, and entertaining experiences *can* occur during meditation, but that is not a requirement and not our goal. Special moments don't have to happen for the experience to have its emotional, physical, or spiritual benefits. But if cool things happen during meditation, hang out and enjoy them. As you immerse more deeply in the experience and drift from the mantra, you will see yourself move from witnessing the experience to thinking about it. As you begin to apply greater meaning to your experience, you will move back into activity from your stillness. At that point, you are essentially back where you started: in activity. That's okay. It's all part of the process. When you realize you have moved back into thought, just gently drift back to the mantra or the object of your attention.

Your meditation session is part of your daily practice. Have you ever been to the gym? Most likely the reason that you go there is to work out . . . to practice. You don't go to the gym to get magically fit in an hour or necessarily to be entertained. Your hour-long sessions at the gym bring you strength, flexibility, and balance throughout the day and night. That's where the benefits of the practice come through. And over time, from those regular one-hour workouts, there is a subtle shift to your body and your emotional state.

The reason you work out is so that when you leave the gym, you are more physically fulfilled in the rest of your life. You're not that concerned with achieving your peak health *in the gym*. The gym is your practice. It's the same thing for yoga classes.

And it's the same for your meditation practice. Those 30-minute sessions are the practice for the rest of your day . . . for the rest of your week . . . for the rest of your life. You aren't serving the world when you're sitting and meditating in the dark. It's when the session is over and you open your eyes and go back with the rest of us that you can be more expansive, more creative, more intuitive, more compassionate, more abundant, more self-loving, and more open to infinite possibilities.

This, of course, is in addition to all the other physical benefits that ripple through your physiology. So nothing special is supposed to happen during the meditation, but when it does, enjoy it; hang out there, and let it soak in. If you have enjoyable experiences, you'll keep coming back. Cool visions and intense sensations can occur during your meditation. You can experience deep energetic and spiritual connections, and you can witness your astral body and even the gap. But those aren't the signs of a successful meditation. A successful meditation is one you *do*. The magic happens when you open your eyes. The benefit happens in every word, every thought, and every action that flows from you as you carry around a little bit of stillness and silence with a dash of pure potentiality. The benefits of meditation happen in your waking state, so don't be looking for clues during the meditation. Just do it!

MYTH #3: I DON'T THINK I'M DOING IT RIGHT.

So many of us perfectionists out there want to know that we are "doing it right."

How many times have we asked ourselves right before, during, and after meditation, "Am I doing it right?" Or because you didn't experience the Buddha or nirvana, because you didn't see colors, because you had thousands of thoughts, you resigned yourself to the fact that you weren't doing it right?

Whenever you ask "Am I doing it right?" the answer is *yes,* you are doing it right! There's more performance anxiety about whether we're doing it right in meditation than any other pressure I can think of. Well now and forever, know that the pressure is off here. In meditation, as long as you are doing it, you're doing it right. Who's your biggest critic? It's you. And judging your meditation practice is no different. There's no need to be so hard on yourself. Don't be critical of your form. Don't try. Release. Let go. Surrender to the unknown. Surrender to what you don't know. Surrender to the fact that you have only one purpose in meditation, and that is to innocently repeat the mantra or follow your breath, depending on which meditation practice you choose.

As long as you do that, you are doing it right. So congratulate yourself for just *doing* it. Don't fret so much about form; just do the practice with innocence. Surrender, and your life will blossom and bloom. After several consecutive days of meditating, you will hear, "Hey, you look more relaxed." Or, "Wow, great idea! I didn't expect that from you." Or, "Hey did you have some work done?" "Is that prescription? Where can I get some of that?" Or, "I want some of what you've got!"

That's your indicator that you're doing it right. And if no one says anything, know that as long as you're doing it, you're doing it right. In time, you will be amazed at how life unfolds and how your awareness of life unfolds with it.

MYTH #4: IF I MEDITATE LONG ENOUGH, I WILL ACHIEVE ENLIGHTENMENT.

In your very essence—at your very core—you were born enlightened, and enlightened you shall die. But from the time you were born into this world, you have been layered with interpretations, perspectives, and conditioning. From each moment since your birth, these layers have covered that wholeness, purity, perfection, and pure consciousness from which you were formed.

You came through that birth canal, and an entire lifetime of conditioning was unveiled to you from the very first moment when the doctor gently patted you on the tush to welcome you into this physical realm. Since that very moment, doctors, nurses, parents, siblings, boyfriends, girlfriends, father figures, teachers, students, mother figures, spouses, exes, coaches, clergy, bosses—and a lifetime of experiences—layered, layered, and layered you with conditioning.

It's a few days, years, decades later, and you've traveled pretty far from that moment of pure, infinite, enlightened perfection. But that pure, infinite, enlightened, perfection is still who you are at your very core, underneath all those layers of conditioning. Meditation allows you to see glimpses of your pure, unconditioned, universal self and, therefore, have a deeper understanding of your life and perhaps life itself.

Will you become enlightened? That is the wrong question. You already are. You simply may not be awake to it. But each time you meditate, you get an opportunity to reach back and peel away more layers of that lifetime of conditioning. And you get to dip your toes in, dip your fingers in . . . and reconnect to your unconditioned self—your pure, whole, perfect, enlightened self. And each time you dip your toes in, you bring back a *thimbleful* of stillness; each time you dip your fingers in, you bring back a *tweezer full* of silence; each time you surrender to who you really are in meditation, you take back an *eyedropper full* of your unconditioned self. Back into each day, back into each moment, back into each breath. So will you become enlightened? It's the wrong question. You already are. Will you awaken yourself to your wholeness? Yes. Meditation by meditation, moment by moment, you will wake up to more of your enlightened self.

MYTH #5: IF I MEDITATE, I AM A SUPERIOR HUMAN BEING, BECAUSE I AM SPIRITUAL.

Meditation is a gift . . . a gift that you give yourself each time you practice. It's also a gift that you give to the world around you. There is no spiritual hierarchy of humans based on whether they meditate or for how long. This is a spurious claim used by insecure individuals under the guise of spiritual expertise. This is the same claim that fundamentalists of all religions and belief systems have used for millennia to elevate themselves and distance nonfollowers. I do not believe meditation embraces a spiritual hierarchy. I believe it embraces the Golden Rule.

Having a daily meditation practice doesn't make someone better than anyone else. Meditation allows you to connect more deeply and more frequently to your source . . . your highest power

. . . your universality . . . the stillness and silence that rests within each of us . . . your most unconditioned self. The more you can tap into your unconditioned self—that pure, unbounded, divine aspect of yourself—the easier it is to see your universality, which is essentially seeing yourself in others and seeing others in yourself. In that state of one-ness awareness, there is no comparison between you and anyone else.

NAMASTÉ
I HONOR THE DIVINE IN YOU

Namasté (pronounced "nahmah-stay," with the emphasis on the last syllable) is a Sanskrit word meaning "I honor the divine place in you that is also in me. And I know that when you are in that space and I am in that space that we are one." Namasté is used as a traditional salutation when greeting someone (similar to shalom, aloha, and assalamu alaikum) and saying good-bye. It's used as a way to herald the universal essence—the one-ness—that connects two people.

The last time I checked, there were close to 8 billion people on the planet. At the end of our lives, when we leave this earthly existence and reach the pearly gates, top of the mountain, or wherever we are going, we will see that there are 8 billion paths to get there. Ours was only one path of the billions that exist.

If it works for you . . . do it. But neither a meditation practice, a yoga practice, nor a religious practice will make you superior to anyone else. In fact, these teachings state that you are neither above nor below anyone else. Each relationship is simply a mirror of yourself. In Sanskrit, the sutra *tat tvam asi* means "You are that." Whatever you judge in another person is a reflection of you, what you recoil from is what you'd like less of in yourself, and what you praise in others is an aspect within you that you praise and often desire more of. I believe our words, thoughts, and actions in our daily life—the threads of our relationships—are the criteria to which we should pay attention, not how much time we spend sitting in darkness and repeating a mantra. To determine what kind of person you are, listen to the answers to these questions:

Are you aware of your impact on others? On yourself? Are you forgiving? To others? To yourself? Have you learned from your pain? Are you compassionate and kind? Do you realize the power of your wake? Can you learn from unanticipated uncertainties in your life? Can you grow from struggle? Can you embrace your ego? Can you embrace your own unconditional love? Do you leave ojas (sweet nectar) instead of ama (toxic residue) when you exit a room, a job, a relationship, this life? And what do you do once you realize that you have left ama?

Whether you meditate, practice yoga, or are deeply devoted to some divine being, you will still be human and subject to all the vagaries, challenges, and opportunities that humans face each day in their bodies, their minds, and their souls. Buddhist teacher and philosopher Jack Kornfield wrote his book *After the Ecstasy, the Laundry: How the Heart Grows Wise on the Spiritual Path* to help reinforce that we are all sentient beings just trying to get by and sharing the best each of us has to offer every day. A regular meditation practice can help you enjoy and appreciate the life you currently live and take it to an even deeper level of fulfillment.

CHAPTER FOURTEEN

CULTIVATING A DAILY MEDITATION PRACTICE

"The practice of mindfulness begins in the small, remote cave of your unconscious mind and blossoms with the sunlight of your conscious life, reaching far beyond the people and places you can see."

— EARON DAVIS

If you can commit to meditating for 30 minutes every day for 21 days straight, your life will change forever, and you will want to meditate every day for the rest of your life. Following the guidance contained in this book can help you start your practice if you've never meditated or to reengage if you have drifted away from your practice. But in the end, *you* have to see the value, so you will want to continue on a daily basis. Make a commitment today; give yourself three weeks to allow the practice to settle in comfortably. Most likely you will miss a meditation here or there. Just pick up the next day, and you'll still feel the cumulative results. Try not to miss consecutive days. Are you ready to take your life to the next level? You can start right now.

Most people who slip away from a meditation practice become crisis meditators. They know the value of the practice, but they have stopped meditating for some reason. Then when they begin interpreting their life as filled with challenges, they turn to meditation for a few days, weeks, or months.

There's a big difference between meditating once in a while and having a meditation practice. Having a practice is when you can successfully string together consecutive days of meditation until it is ritualized. Ideally, this will become part of your daily routine, no different than brushing your teeth. So why is it so hard?

It's really not. Yet former meditators cite two main reasons for why they stop a perfectly fulfilling practice after only a few days or weeks: lack of time and subtlety of results.

Excuse #1: I Don't Have Enough Time

The number one excuse people give for not meditating is that they don't have enough time. They have time for watching TV, surfing the net, texting, talking, watching movies, writing, hobbies, playing Wii, working late, partying, reading, relaxing, checking e-mails, cooking meals, Facebooking, bathing, napping, commuting, waiting, flying, Tweeting, waiting, brushing, playing with the dog, taking care of the baby, seeing the doctor, waiting, hurrying up, and waiting. We determine what activities we fit into each moment of the 24 hours of our day. Of course you have the time to meditate for 30 minutes every day, even if you just shaved one minute from each of your morning activities. Time is not some independent being that imposes itself on our schedule. We develop our schedule based on our values and beliefs. We decide what we think is the best use of our life energy and how much time we are willing to allot to various activities.

What I have found is that when you incorporate a meditation practice into your life, suddenly there is time for everything. You approach everything from a point of greater clarity and ease. Deadlines evaporate as you finish projects ahead of schedule. You experience more restful sleep, which gives you greater vitality and the ability to focus. You become more efficient in all your work, so there is finally some free time and some breathing room. You realize the non-nourishing behaviors you were expending energy on, and you are able to replace them with more nourishing, more efficient behaviors—ways of living that support you more. But you have to take the step first, so I suggest that you commit to a week or two or three of a daily meditation practice, and you will see how the time in your life expands to fit everything you want . . . and more.

Excuse #2: I Don't Feel the Results

The second most common reason people cite for not meditating is that they think the results are too subtle, so they can't see any value in continuing. Again, this goes back to our misconceptions about what meditation is supposed to be. If your expectations are to levitate and see colors but you are only aware of drifting back and forth between the mantra and thoughts, you will assume it's not working and give up. You may even think you're doing it wrong, because you don't have any aha! moments during your practice.

Remember, the benefits happen in the other 23 hours in the day, when we are not meditating. So be patient and stop looking for the higher state of consciousness to arrive. It will flow into you when it is time, so don't worry or be concerned. Just keep meditating, and after a few weeks, you will recognize distinct changes in the way you interact with life, stress, disappointments, unmet needs, and your own thoughts.

Having a meditation practice is no different than doing some form of physical exercise every day. Exercise subtly tightens your body; meditating every day gently eases your mind into a sense of well-being. Why wouldn't you want to do the same thing for your emotional state, your physical body, and your spiritual possibilities?

In order to bring this peace and stillness into your life on a daily basis, you must have a practice that supports the process. So many of us have meditated either through a guided meditation tape or CD, lying on our backs in savasana at the end of a yoga class, or simply sitting in silence for a few minutes. Each of these experiences brings a sense of calm to our lives, but they don't necessarily shift our consciousness over the long term. Changing the way we view the world, our life, others' words and actions, and our own behavior requires a shift in our pattern of behavior.

To achieve this shift, you must dip into that stillness and silence on a regular basis. The optimal duration is 30 minutes, and the ideal frequency is twice each day—once in the morning and once in the afternoon or evening.

Feel free to use any of the mantras mentioned throughout this book. Find one that resonates with you, and use it consistently for 21 days. Use one mantra and stay with it. If you change the mantra too often, it will end up creating thought and activity. Remember, we use the mantra to disconnect us from activity, so don't feel the need to synchronize your breathing to the vibrations of the mantra. If you determine that you'd like to use a mantra, there are some classic universal sounds, including the traditional mantra *Om,* the *so hum* mantra that Deepak Chopra has popularized worldwide for more than 20 years, and the mantra we used in the *I Am* meditation, or any of the other mantras I've shared.

Feel free to use any of those or any you find online; and if you'd like to personalize your practice, find a certified meditation instructor near you. You can e-mail me at **secrets@davidji.com**, and we can discuss the best way for you to receive your primordial sound mantra where you live.

If you'd prefer to simply follow your breath, make sure that you don't force the breath; just let it flow. Simply follow your breath in and out. You will do this for approximately 30 minutes. Whichever method you choose to meditate, I've recorded several free meditation timers that you can download from **davidji.com** onto your iPhone, iPad, iPod, BlackBerry, Droid, tablet, or right onto your computer. They are perfect meditation timers and give you the option of 5-, 10-, 15-, 20-, 25-, or 30-minute meditations.

Over time, the method you use can shift and evolve. So keep an open mind and stay with the practice.

The Exception to the Rule

Many schools of meditation perform certain rituals before the actual meditation occurs, such as chanting Om, saying a prayer, setting intentions, or asking questions. The purpose is not to then bring these questions actively into your meditation. In fact, it's to get certain intentions and dialogues out into the ether. I like the question-and-answer format prior to meditation, because it allows me the opportunity to settle into the key things going on in my life and to bring some intentions—not just my attention—to them.

New meditators who are high achievers often apply that same level of effort, focus, and concentration that they have applied to every other aspect of their life. It usually brings results in our world, and their track record might be brilliant. In fact, most of us were taught the following equation at a very young age:

Focus + Effort = Success

We were also taught that if we increase the effort, the level of success will expand as well. The lesson we absorbed was: work hard enough, and we can have everything we want. For many of us, that's how we achieved everything we cherish, which only reinforced the belief system that focus and effort were the key ingredients to any success. But as you may have noticed, this supposed law of life doesn't always apply to every aspect of life. In fact, in time it becomes more of a personal style—a way we live our life—rather than a law that we consciously follow. But this "natural" law of our society doesn't always translate life's challenges into expansive solutions. By coming from a different perspective or withdrawing so fully and then re-immersing, we sometimes see something once familiar with a new set of "eyes," infinitely increasing the possibilities for expansion and growth.

In meditation, it's the exception to the rule that brings us success. The best results occur when we let go of all effort . . . to the point of surrender . . . total melting, total softening. We let go of focus, replacing it with innocence—and the innocent repetition of the mantra. The formula for an effective meditation is:

Surrender + Innocence = Success

It goes against everything we've been taught. Surrendering is counterintuitive for successful, accomplished, or powerful individuals who have *worked* hard to achieve all their positions and possessions. All that you've accomplished in this life is based on DOing. Meditation is about BEing. So you require a different set of tools to connect with your divine inner self that rests beneath all of these positions and possessions—to just BE.

Asking the Soul Questions

You can begin your daily practice with any questions or any prayer you feel like starting with. In the practice of Primordial Sound Meditation, we often begin by asking ourselves a series of questions known as the soul questions. But regardless of what type of meditation style you practice, you can still begin your daily meditation by asking yourself these powerful and profound questions. They are explored in greater depth in the book *The Seven Spiritual Laws of Yoga.* The questions are *Who am I? What do I want?* and *What is my dharma or purpose in life?* These are the questions that hundreds of thousands of Primordial Sound Meditation practitioners ask themselves before they begin repeating their mantras.

And it is by asking these questions, listening to answers, and then letting go of outcomes that we begin our daily practice. ***There is no need to bring the questions or the answers into your mind during the meditation.*** They are already a part of who you are. And as you expand in consciousness, the cosmic dialogue will continue to expand within you, and you will gain clarity into who you are, you will receive all that you desire, and you will discover your purpose for being here. (Remember: Don't bring any thoughts, concepts, ideas, plans, or expectations into the meditation—only your mantra.)

These are some of the deepest questions you could ask yourself, which is why we do nothing with the information that comes to us during meditation. That's simply a process for making the soil more fertile. It's outside of meditation, when the seeds you've planted are growing, that you feel more expanded, more creative, more intuitive, and more insightful. It's not during meditation that the value of this process takes form. It's back here with the rest of us, when you're eyes are wide open, and you're interacting with the world.

Who am I? What do I want? What's my dharma or purpose? How can I help, heal, and serve others using my unique gifts and my special talents? These are the stepping-stones to an effortless daily practice, and they are the building blocks for living my life. Of course, you can begin your practice with any ritual that feels comfortable. What are the questions that are important to you? Write them down, explore them before meditating for a solid week, and you will feel them unfold in your life. (Remember: Don't bring these questions or their answers into your meditation.) *After you have asked and answered (and sometimes there will be no answers) all these questions, simply release them.* You can add emphasis to your letting go of them by physically releasing them. Take a long, slow, deep breath in and then let them go. As you exhale, send them out into the universe. Then begin your practice, using your breath, mantra, or another object of your attention.

When Should I Meditate?

In the era when these teachings were first made popular, almost 5,000 years ago, most people were farmers. They rose before sunrise, they washed, they prayed and meditated, and then they went into the fields at the first hint of sunrise. They worked in the fields with their animals and then they retired for the day before sunset. They meditated before dinner, and they slept as the sun slept. For more than 5,000 years, Ayurveda has taught that the ideal times to meditate are between the hours of 5 and 7 A.M. and between 5 and 7 P.M. According to Ayurveda, these times of the day are at the lightest part of the morning and evening (the end of vata time: 2–6). This, of course, corresponds to the rising and setting of the sun, which is how these ancient civilizations guided their lives. Ayurveda was developed long before Las Vegas and eBay . . . long before night shifts, nightclubs, swing shifts, and round-the-clock emergency rooms, and long before planes, trains, and buses moved through the night . . . long before nocturnal behaviors began to buck the natural circadian rhythms of nature. So this ancient guidance had little knowledge that we would be living in an age where people went out to dinner when it was already dark, and many of us rose long after the sun had come up.

The Power of Ritual

So when is the right time? I used to say to myself, *I'll meditate at ten o clock every morning.* But ten never comes. You know what it's like. The phone rings. The dog needs attention. You suddenly are greeted with information that requires attention. You spend more time than you thought you would on sending an e-mail, going to a store, or dealing with a challenge. And then it's noon, and you have a lunch meeting. You plan for three o'clock but then you get pulled away, so you promise yourself you will meditate as soon as you get home. But a friend calls and asks you out to dinner. And then you go to a movie and then to a club for dancing, and before you know it, it's midnight and you haven't meditated.

If you lock your meditation in like a seamless ritual, it will just flow without thought. We create and maintain behaviors by ritualizing them. The easiest way to lock in your daily meditation practice—and most important, your morning meditation—is to ritualize it. Make it part of a series of activities that you do based on each activity flowing from one into the other, rather than what time it is while you're performing them.

For example, when you wake up each morning you look at the clock—then you pee. You don't say to yourself, "It's 6:30; time to pee." That happens as a natural flow of your morning ritual. Then you do the next thing on your invisible list of morning activities and then the next. For most people, they pretty much do the same things in the same order every day. We create behaviors and maintain behaviors by ritualizing them. You don't know what time you brush your teeth every morning, because you don't do it based on time; you do it based on following some order of rituals you've created over the years. It's only one of your morning ablution rituals. We have between 8 and 15 that we deploy in a certain sequence on waking. Sometimes we have a different ritual for the weekends and one for the workweek. They evolve over time, but each of us has this autopilot string of rituals we perform each day like clockwork.

You don't brush at a particular time, but you always brush after a particular morning ablution activity and before you engage in another. It starts when you wake up; perhaps by alarm, the sun, or maybe you just wake up. The next thing you do is look at the clock to orient yourself. Then you do 1 of these 15 activities in the same ritualistic order you always do, and you do them all like a prearranged dance. You *wake;* you *pee;* you *wash* your face; you *move your bowels;* you *shower;* you *groom* yourself by *shaving* or putting on *makeup;* you do your *hair;* you *dress;* you tend to your *cat, dog, bird,* or *snake;* you tend to any *children* or *babies* in the house; you *interact* with your significant or insignificant *other;* you watch morning *TV;* you read a *newspaper;* you go *online;* you have *sex;* you make *coffee* or *tea;* and you *eat* or serve some form of breakfast. And each day, you perform these activities in the same ritualistic order, on autopilot, every day for months, years, even decades.

The Effortless Ritual: RPM

To solve the difficulty that most meditators have ensuring that they lock in that first meditation of the day, I developed a ritual that has helped thousands effortlessly lock down their practice. It's known as RPM, which stands for Rise, Pee, Meditate. It's based on the fact that you wake up each day. So what time do you wake up?

It's not too big a leap to think that within a few minutes of waking, you're going to pee. Well, you're two-thirds of the way there! If the very next thing you do is sit down to meditate, then within 35 minutes of opening your eyes in the morning, you'll have a half-hour of stillness and silence inside you to greet every moment as you move throughout the rest of your day.

You will be more relaxed regardless of what you face throughout the day. You'll be less reactive. More reflective and less reflexive. More creative. More intuitive. More compassionate.

More understanding. And more alert. All that within 35 minutes of opening your eyes. In the first few minutes after you wake up, you have the least amount of active thoughts, but the flow of making meaning out of each moment as you get further into the day quickly accelerates your mind's activity. If the first thing you do when you wake up is meditate, then logically, there will be fewer distractions to begin the practice. What time do you wake up: four, five, six, seven, eight, nine, ten? What time do you start your job? Do you work a normal schedule, or do you work swing shift? Do you work in an emergency room? Does your schedule buck the natural rhythms of nature? How many hours are there between the time you wake up and when you leave your house? And what do you do with that time? How much time is spent reading a paper, watching TV, or going online? Couldn't you take a few minutes from each of your morning ablution rituals and wake up 15 minutes earlier?

There, you'd have that sweet unhurried 30 minutes to start your day. If the answer is no, then revisit what time you go to bed and try going to sleep 15 minutes earlier for a few weeks in a row. It will suddenly be a part of who you are. You can make this work. Then you will ease effortlessly into this morning ritual as easily as you did into the rituals of watching TV, brushing your teeth, making your morning brew, or taking your morning walk. Pushing RPM to the very front of your morning ablution ritual train will allow you to integrate it into your daily routine until it is as much a part of your morning flow as any of your other morning ablution rituals. So yes, Ayurveda says to meditate between the hours of five and seven, but you have to do what works best for you. The key is to create a ritual.

The evening is more difficult, because now you have time issues on both sides of your meditation practice, and your mind is very active. For the afternoon or evening meditation, I suggest the acronym RAW (Right After Work). Make it the very, very, very last thing you do before you leave work or the very, very, very first thing you do when you get home. This way it's ritualized, and there aren't any time pressures.

If you meditate using the RAW ritual, you will ever so gently coast into your evening before it explodes with activity: dinner, kids, stories of the day, TV, Internet, pets, workouts, and anything else you cram into those last remaining hours you are awake. You will be bringing a bit of stillness and silence into the activity. And you will be in alignment with the timeless wisdom of Ayurveda as well as the circadian rhythms of nature. If you can have your evening meditation under your belt, you handle it all with grace and aplomb. If it feels better for you to meditate closer to your bedtime, do that. Just remember meditating too close to bedtime will "steal" your sleep, rejuvenating you so much that you may have trouble getting to bed. Maintain this philosophy: When it comes to your afternoon or evening meditation, do whatever works!

Where Should I Meditate?

I meditate each morning on a fat, round, zafu pillow with my dog Peaches the Buddha Princess curled up on a zafu right next to me. (She has her own Facebook page! Please like her.) I sit in front of a coffee table that I place a digital clock on. I don't use a timer or alarm. I meditate and open my eyes when I am aware I'm thinking about time. I glance at the clock, take in the time, and go back into meditation. What should you do? First, leave your bed. Find a spot that you don't connect with other ritualized behaviors. Try not to start off lying down; it will create a Pavlovian connection between sleep and meditation. Pick any relatively quiet place where you can be relaxed and comfortable. In extreme circumstances, meditators have meditated in their bathrooms, their cars, even their closets. But that shouldn't be necessary. Find a quiet spot that feels somewhat sacred or special, a place you can imagine sitting in every day, and find a cushion, pillow, or chair that you can relax in for at least 30 minutes. Move toward the most comfortable seat and the most comfortable position. Always keep moving toward comfort, wherever that is.

Feel free to meditate while commuting (as long as you are not driving), at the doctor's office, in the airport, at a sporting event, at a rock concert, or during any long trip you are taking. The next time you have five free minutes, see what it feels like to use those precious minutes tapping into the stillness and silence that rests within. It doesn't matter what direction you face: God is everywhere. I like to face east to feel the first light of morning come into my meditation. I feel the light come in, and I smile. Usually this is followed by hearing birds, but every day is different . . . all so special. If you need to peek, peek. If you need to move, move. If you need to stretch, stretch. Do whatever you need to do: sneeze, cough, yawn, yelp. Always move toward comfort. If you are pulled out of meditation by some disturbance, tend to your urgent situation and then return and meditate for the remaining minutes.

If for any reason you find that you have skipped a day or a meditation, give yourself a hug for noticing. Cut yourself some slack and then dive right back in. The practice is cumulative, so don't worry if you slip away as long as you are willing to slip back in.

The Ten-and-a-Half Most Valuable Keys to a Successful Daily Practice

Whether you meditate using your breath or using a mantra as the object of your attention, there are several keys to an effortless and comfortable daily practice:

1. **Comfort is queen.** Make sure you are comfortable in every moment. If you're comfortable, you'll continue to meditate; if you're not comfortable, most likely you'll stop. So no matter what the disturbance, don't resist; stop and deal with it (stretch your legs, look at your watch, rub your neck, turn off your phone, scratch your cheek), and drift back to the mantra.

2. **Create a ritual.** Don't pin your meditation to a time on the clock. Use a ritual such as RPM (Rise, Pee, Meditate) or any other ritual that works for you. The afternoon ritual can be RAW (Right After Work) or any other ritual that feels comfortable. Allow your 30 minutes to be sacred. Remember: Whatever works.

3. **Remember to let go.** Ask your questions and set your intentions innocently before you meditate and then let go of them. Don't bring anything into the meditation other than the mantra or the object of attention. When you notice these thoughts, drift back.

4. **Stay innocent.** Bring nothing into the meditation other than the object of your attention—your mantra or your breath. Do not have an intention, agenda, or target that you bring into the meditation. Don't force your practice. Let it innocently unfold.

5. **Witness.** Let go of any expectations you may have about the practice. Nothing is *supposed* to happen. Observe whatever flows into you . . . and drift back to the mantra. Don't start journaling . . . just witness.

6. **Keep drifting.** Treat any interruption, sound, old mantra, idea, mood, feeling, or emotion as you would any other thought; and gently drift back to the object of your attention: the mantra or your breath.

7. **Let go of meaning.** Don't get distracted with the meaning of any sutra or mantra. Use your mantra for its vibrational quality; the meaning will take care of itself.

8. **Surrender.** Repeat your mantra effortlessly, like mist rising off a lake at dawn.

9. **Listen to your mantra.** Don't say your mantra; *listen* to it. Let it bubble up.

10.   **You are perfect.** Whatever happens is perfect! Do not judge the experience. Every meditation is like a snowflake, unique and never to be repeated.

10½. **Enjoy!** Don't get too serious. This is a lighthearted practice, so have fun.

CHAPTER FIFTEEN

Frequently Asked Questions

"There is no God other than life itself."

— Osho

There are thousands of frequently asked questions regarding what one experiences during meditation, and I have addressed the most frequent of the frequent. The simple fact remains that the answer to every question rests within you. Simply meditate, follow the guidance in this book, and when you have a question, the answer will most likely come from inside. And if it doesn't, e-mail me your challenge, and we can figure it out together. So before you ask any questions, just meditate every day for 30 minutes in the morning and 30 minutes in the afternoon or evening. Start by asking a few questions, meditate in silence, end the silence with an alarm or a chime, and then seal the meditation with an "Om."

After you have done this for three weeks, your life will be different, and you will then be able to ask yourself, *Do I like my life more when I'm meditating or more when I'm not meditating?*

If you like it more, keep going, and your life will continue to blossom and bloom. If you aren't sure, keep meditating for another 21 days. After you hit your 21st day, send me an e-mail at **secrets@ davidji.com** and tell me how it feels and what's gone on in your life. Tell me your challenges and your triumphs. Ask any questions you'd like, and I'll personally reply to you.

If you don't feel that 21 days of meditation has provided any value in your life, pass this book on to someone else. Send me an e-mail, and let's chat about it before you decide to move on.

What's the difference between prayer and meditation?

Prayer is talking to God . . . meditation is listening. Quiet yourself through meditation, and you will connect more deeply to whatever god you pray to. Quiet yourself and you will hear the whispers of the Divine.

How can I tell if I'm ready to embark on a spiritual journey or attend a meditation workshop?

We've all heard the saying, "When the student is ready, the teacher appears." When people begin asking themselves whether they'd benefit from a more intense inner journey, they are usually ready. At a meditation retreat, most attendees are like-minded in terms of being open to the concepts of expanded states of consciousness and deeper states of peace. The energy of the collective is tangible and can be an empowering experience to help you take bolder steps in your life. If that sounds overwhelming, start more slowly and learn to meditate with a teacher in a more intimate environment. I work one-on-one and with groups to help individuals cultivate a spiritual practice. I travel the world teaching at retreats, workshops, and seminars. If you'd like to start or deepen your practice, reach out to me and we can chat about your next steps.

What should my goal be during meditation?

It's paradoxical but your goal is to simply *be* . . . not *do.* So depending upon the type of meditation you choose, just do that. For example, in mantra meditation, just repeat the mantra. In breath awareness, just breathe. In drishti meditation, just gaze. It's a rookie mistake to try to intellectualize or add *anything* to the process. Simpler is better. Less is more.

Where do I find a teacher?

The ideal way to learn mantra meditation is still directly from a practicing teacher. They don't have to wear monks' robes or Indian saris to teach you. My criteria are that they meditate daily and use mantra meditation effectively in their life. If so, they can share the practice with you and support you. Feel free to visit **davidji.com**'s meditation resource page to find a teacher near you.

What mantra should I use to start?

Select a mantra you will feel comfortable with—not for its supposed meaning, but from its vibration alone. Feel free to use any of the mantras listed below, or learn your personal mantra through a certified meditation teacher. Visit **davidji.com** for more information. In the meantime, the following mantras can work very effectively until you receive your Primordial Sound Mantra:

> *I Am*
> *So Hum*
> *Om*
> *Yud Hey Vov Hey*
> *Aham Brahmasmi* or any of *the mahavakyas*
> *Om Ganapati Namah*
> *Yogastha Kuru Karmani*
> *Moksha*
> *Om Mani Padme Hum*
> *TRUST*
> *Om Namah Shivaya*
> *So Hum Namah*

Should I try to synchronize the mantra with my breath?

This is another trap for those who have practiced a form of breathing meditation who then try to use a mantra. When you breathe as the object of your attention, your breath rises and falls, speeds and slows . . . the same thing happens to the mantra. They will diverge at some point, sort of like rubbing your belly and patting your head. So there is no way to really synchronize or coordinate the two. If you have a breath-awareness practice and you want to move to a mantra-based practice, try synching your breath and the mantra for a few minutes and then *let go* of the breath and solely drift your attention to the mantra.

Can I listen to soothing meditation or yoga music during the meditation?

You can do anything you like, *but* if you use music during your meditation practice, you are staying in activity. The reason you like music is that it soothes and relaxes you. But it also reminds you of something relaxing and therefore you are introducing meaning to the meditation, which will drift you into thought. My strong suggestion is that the only way to experience pure unbounded consciousness is through stillness. *Yogastha kuru karmani!* Established in presence, perform action. If you can create stillness as the bookends of your day, then add any other kind of meditation or practice in between. That practice will soar as long as you bracket it with experiences of no-activity.

I fell off the wagon and stopped meditating. Help!

First of all, take a deep breath right now. Life can get busy and sometimes feel overwhelming. This can create a domino effect in which certain "noncritical" daily rituals get dropped. This simply means that you have chosen to allocate 30 minutes to another activity in your day over the perceived value of meditation in your life. You have certain expectations, and you're not feeling the results, so you don't see the value. That's a common response from those who stop practicing meditation. But if you want to, you can easily reconnect with your most centered self, starting now.

You can gently drift back to your practice today by selecting a few moments to celebrate that you are even having this conversation. Pick a time today . . . anytime throughout the day . . . when you can dedicate 10 minutes and work your way up to 30 minutes by increasing 1 minute per day. Don't feel constrained or pressured, but make sure that you truly dedicate your attention and intention to this gift that you are giving yourself.

AFTERWORD

Meditating every day has opened my world to lean more deeply in the direction of my dreams and away from what no longer serves me. It's a process and a lifelong journey. I am now aware when words leave my lips that don't create peace and harmony. I'm now aware when I have thoughts that really don't serve me. Meditation has awakened the silent witness within me, and that has made all the difference. I am less reactive, more compassionate, more forgiving of myself and others, happier and more fulfilled . . . and I feel truly blessed to walk on this sweet earth.

I believe this comes from seeing the daily benefits and results of this practice. I look forward to connecting to the stillness and silence that rests within, because I now know it is the source of all existence.

You are not alone on this journey. We are all together, stumbling through each day to put some food in our bellies and receive love. In the process, we can share love, light, acceptance, forgiveness, encouragement, and peace with everyone we touch.

If we can do this—even just a bit more than we did yesterday—then this life of ours, as transient and uncertain as it is, will be the most amazing journey one could ever fathom.

I have become more sensitive to the obligation we each have to nurture and protect all the sentient beings on the planet. This includes animals in shelters and on factory farms, wild game, our beautiful oceans and the life that teems within, and the brave military veterans and their families who have served and sacrificed so we could have one more day of freedom. I hope one day we can all live in peace, so none of their sacrifices will be in vain. Remember to love thy neighbor and adopt your next pet. Visit **davidji.com** to connect with me and more of these timeless teachings.

MY INTENTIONS

What is your reasoning behind establishing a daily meditation practice? What are your expectations? Write them down here or in your journal and date it. Then check back every month, and you'll see how you've manifested these desires in your life!

_____

_____

_____

_____

_____

_____

_____

_____

My Experiences During and Outside of Meditation

As your thoughts, breath, and physiology slow and progressively quiet to more subtle expressions, your awareness will expand—at first during meditation and then in your life outside of meditation—which will awaken a world of infinite possibilities in every moment. Write down your experiences and realizations here or in your journal, and you'll see the ways in which you've positively transformed your life.

_____

_____

_____

_____

_____

_____

_____

_____

_____

RECOMMENDED READING

Adi Shankara's Crest Jewel of Discrimination: Timeless Teachings on Nonduality. Swami Prabhavananda and Christopher Isherwood, translators. Hollywood, CA: Vedanta Press, 1975.

Chödrön, Pema. *When Things Fall Apart: Heart Advice for Difficult Times.* Boston: Shambhala Library, 1997.

Chopra, Deepak. *The Way of the Wizard.* New York: Harmony Books, 1995.

Chopra, Deepak. *The Spontaneous Fulfillment of Desire: Harnessing the Infinite Power of Coincidence.* New York: Harmony Books, 2003.

Chopra, Deepak, and Simon, David. *The Seven Spiritual Laws of Yoga: A Practical Guide to Healing Body, Mind, and Spirit.* Hoboken, NJ: John Wiley & Sons, 2004.

Houston, Jean. *A Mythic Life: Learning to Live Our Greater Story.* San Francisco: Harper San Francisco, 1996.

Ladinsky, Daniel (translator). *The Gift: Poems by Hafiz, the Great Sufi Master.* New York: Penguin Books, 1999.

Rosenberg, Marshall B. *Nonviolent Communication: A Language of Life.* Encinitas, CA: PuddleDancer Press, 2003.

Shearer, Alistair (translation and introduction). *The Yoga Sutras of Patanjali.* New York: Random House, 1982.

Simon, David. *The Ten Commitments: Translating Good Intentions into Great Choices.* Deerfield Beach, FL: Heath Communications, 2006.

Simon, David. *Free to Love, Free to Heal: Healing Your Body by Healing Your Emotions.* Carlsbad, CA: Chopra Center Press, 2009.

Yogananda, Paramahansa. *Autobiography of a Yogi.* Los Angeles: Self-Realization Fellowship, 1997.

IN GRATITUDE

Ollie, Eddie, Annie, Francis, Monroe, and sweet Mazy. Meditating in the nonlocal. You are my daily spirit guides. Shanti, shalom, and peace.

Deepak Chopra swirls the heavens, and David Simon brings heaven to earth. Aham brahmasmi—I am the universe.

Deepak Chopra was the first teacher who taught me to access the answer to the questions *Who am I? What do I want?* and *What is my dharma?* I am forever grateful for his willingness to share with me his brilliance, his passion, his creativity, his articulation, and his compassion. He has brought about more peace on this planet in his life than any other soul; his ability to powerfully connect with people of every culture, age, and orientation is extraordinary. He is an archetypal embodiment of the teachings of Vedanta, Advaita, yoga, and cosmic consciousness; and he has selflessly, gracefully, and prolifically offered this timeless body of wisdom to the world for more than 40 years. I feel honored to be a recipient of that offering for the past decade.

David Simon saw something inside me and invited me into his heart. There I have stayed since the day we met. And there I will stay until I leave this earth. He has guided me through darkness into light and from pain and constriction to moksha—emotional freedom. And it has been my privilege to serve his vision of global healing through higher consciousness and love.

My dear teachers Osho, Paramahansa Yogananda, His Holiness the 14th Dali Lama, Yogi Bhajan, and Roger Gabriel—you move me each day to live a life of greater service, peace, creativity, acceptance, expansion, humor, compassion, love, and abundance.

Rosanne Drucker, my loving wife, brilliant musician/singer/songwriter, and true believer. You've known me a very long time, and through it all, you have always encouraged my next step, no matter how difficult or random it seemed. You believed in me when I could not see my own light, and that has made all the difference.

Your generosity of spirit has been the dharma beacon I have chased all these years. Your creativity, verve, and ability to flow the emotions of the universe into music and lyrics are unparalleled. Your unwavering open heart and your unconditional love have given me the freedom to explore the universe, and in that journey, I have found my soul. There could be no greater gift than your expanded being. Thank you . . . again and forever.

Peaches, the Buddha Princess, you are a living meditation and my unconditional companion who teaches me surrender in each moment and reminds me every day to open my heart just a little bit more.

Tiffany Murray, the "good wife," you are the embodiment of grace under fire. Your devotion to—and seamless integration of—the teachings of the Chopra Center make you the role model for all Vedic Masters to follow. Your selfless service and commitment to authenticity shines through each day, lighting my world and gifting our guests and your students with heartfelt, seasoned, and real-world teachings. You walk the talk, effortlessly gliding past drama and constriction to the island of calm and clarity, and you lovingly share that with all of us. Finding your dharma has helped thousands reconnect to their unconditioned selves, to illumination, and to wholeness. You have elegantly gifted my world and so many others with depth and joy.

Michael Bloom, my dear friend, brother, and guide who understands the true meaning of enlightenment and the power of the present moment—you rock!

My human family that has made it all possible to evolve each day into the best version of myself: my amazing dad and best friend, Jay Greenspan; and his devoted wife, Charna Glasser; the greatest clarinetist who ever breathed life into a licorice stick, Stanley Drucker; my unconditional loving mother Naomi Drucker; my beloved sister, Susie, who has stuck by my side since I ventured out of the womb; my truly authentic brother, Jeffrey; and my soul nephew, Eddie Gilbert. You all have held space for me in my darkest abysses, championed my climbs, and celebrated with me on the peaks. I always feel your love and support regardless of where I am on my journey. I love you dearly.

My amazing sisters who comprise Chopra Center University. You shine the brightest light so millions around the world can move out of the darkness: My partners in taking CCU to the next level—Yogi Claire Diab, director Teresa Long, and developer of online content Tiffany Murray; and our magical team of Erica Lopez, Trista Thorp, Andrea Debell, and Marcella Mighty Morfin.

Karla Refoxo, my dear friend, spoiler of Peaches, and teacher of life. You are the embodiment of tender loving-kindness merged with powerful creativity; a sweet, sensitive, divine soul, and a loving meditation teacher. You started it all with your amazing giant Buddha fresco at the Chopra Center in New York. Your vision of the covers of *Secrets of Meditation* and *Guided Meditations* brought deep clarity and excitement to the projects, as did your artistic sensibility. Thank you for bringing your sweet Gallega energy into my world and teaching me to keep dying to the past. You are a blessed Sufi Nagual, a gifted artist, and a trusted heart friend. Tulku rules! **Tulkujewels.com**

The thousand beams of light that make up the global network of Chopra Center–certified instructors. You inspire me each day as you move in the direction of your dharma, helping, healing, and serving others with your light and love.

The more than 50,000 meditation students around the world who have sat in my classes and in my lectures at the Chopra Center, and around the world at Seduction of Spirit, Journey into Healing, Secrets of Enlightenment, Soul of Healing, Perfect Health, and SynchroDestiny.

The hundreds of thousands around the world who have taken a meditation journey with me online, on CD, via iPod, on radio, or in person. You have been with me in the gap, and we have shared the magic of one-ness. You are the driving force behind my consciousness, and I am profoundly grateful.

The hundreds of members of my Chopra Center family from 2003 to the present and those who have been my mile markers of dharma. For all of you who have been my students and my teachers, my friends and my partners in raising the vibration of peace and nurturing, I thank you from the bottom of my heart and soul.

Kathy Bankerd and Susan McCabe for seeing me as an asset to the cause and helping to raise my vibration.

Kyla Stinnett, for your rapier wit, beguiling charm, brilliant editing, deep sensitivity, and tender heart. Working with you at the Chopra Center has been a privilege and a highlight for me. Walking our dogs on the beach and pondering the enigmas of existence are treasures I hold dearly. Sherman is a very lucky Chihuahua.

Carolyn and Felicia Rangel, you hold the universe so brilliantly so Deepak can spin it with grace and ease.

Sara Harvey for your grace and generosity.

The Vancouver tribe of the Chopra Yoga Center and studio director Danielle Mika Nagel.

Nirmala Raniga, my dear friend and the angelic visionary of Paradise Valley Wellness Centre.

Charley Paz for being my steady rock and advisor.

Amanda "Linky" Ringnalda, my event wife for the past six years.

My undying best buddy and kids' yoga expert, Jodi Komitor.

My Hay House family: the goddess Louise Hay, Reid Tracy, and Stacey Smith; my Hay House Radio family—the incomparable Diane Ray and her brilliant engineering team: Kyle, Steve, Joe, Rocky, and Mitch; my show producers Tiffany Murray and Susan McCabe; the *Secrets of Meditation* editorial and design team of Lisa Bernier, Shannon Littrell, Nick Welch, and Christy Salinas; my sweet meditating rock stars Diane, Bryn, and Donna—you guys keep it real!; and my meditation and Ayurveda students at Hay House who keep raising the roof. Hay House Radio rules!

Lubosh Cech, my loving brother. Words can barely express my admiration and respect for you and your creative vision. You are a divine representation of bhakti and a generous and gifted artist. You ensure that every davidji visual expression to the world carries the perfection, elegance, and sweet intention of the source from which it was originally derived. You are a talented and ever-transforming master. I am in your gratitude. **Okodesign studio.com** and **NakedRiverFilms.com**

Tara Lynda Guber, the yogi who taught me to own my impact. Love you, taraji!

Thank you to those along my path who have gifted me with your friendship and helped me better understand life: my oldest friend, partner, and mentor Mark Clemente; my dear heart, mind, and confidante for so many years Anna Chosak; Marianne Pagmar; Dave Goodley; Terri Cole; Max Simon; Rick Dore; Rookie Komitor; Pam, Sara, and Izzy Simon; Benji Moseman; Dr. Valenica Booth Porter; sweet Fran Lambert; Stanley Komitor; Robin Muto; Freddy Leonardo; Alisha Olivier; Judy Perl; Yogini Shambhavi; Naadi Mohan; Michael Price; the spa genius Alexis Ufland; Grace Porter; Neal Tricarico; Allison Slater; Patrick Flanagan; Tal Wilkinfeld; George Bubaris; Ravi Meher; Dr. Suhas Kshirsagar; Deva Premal; Kimberly Willock Pardiwala; General Al Haig; Vamadeva Shastri; Gerard Butler; Jennifer Nicholson; Sadie Drucker; Christina Warner Hill; Tipper Gore; Guru Ganesha; Tony Robbins; Maya Jeffkins; my program consultant, Vedic Master, and yogini extraordinaire Gabrielle Forleo, who stood by me all the way; my amazing, supportive, and authentic friends at the front desk: Mira, Kathy, Blake, Molly, Sheila, Tala, and Tim; my sisters on the LT: Holly, Amanda, Kristy, Sara, and Traci; Corey Booker; Abby "The Heart" Murphy; Sid Ganis; Sant Chatwal; Greg Porter; Denise Reynier; Justin Drucker; Peter Guber; the crew of the *Jayavarman;* Nancy Ganis; Jeffrey Landle; Laura Lawee; Eliza Dushku; the one and only Wendi Cohen; Kids for Peace; Vikram Chatwal; my friends at the Hoffman Institute; Jagatjoti Singh Khalsa; Julie Silverthorn; all my FB friends and fans; my Twitter followers; Cesar Millan; Ann Lagano; Robert Gonzalez; David Clark; the sweet and talented family at the Chopra Center in New York and the radiant guiding lights who made it happen—Holly Hatfield-Patel and Kerry Williams Gil; Bill Farley; Rick Fox; Chants and Drums; Sarito Sun; Zrii Nation; Charley Paz, Mitch Estrin; Lee Rocker; Katia Shokrai; Irene Margolis; Freddie and Irene Gentile; Dave Macek and the supportive family at Red Lotus Society; Valerie Skonie and the tribe of the 40-day Winter

Feast for the Soul; Bob Budlow; Joshua "Ganesh" Mallitt; Denise Reynier; Dave Stewart; Suzanne Dore; Miten; my roomie and hair twin sistah Lizzie Upitis; Elaine Ehrenkrantz; Jerry Kaplan; Debbie Drucker; my longtime, loving friend, force of nature, and CBGB's partner Amy Berko Iles; Snatam Kaur; Damien Rose; Gail Hendrix; Nicole Bondurant; Libby Carstensen; and my dear Bloomfield brothers—Joe, Ray, Eddie, Walter, and Ted.

And profound thanks to those who have shown me the magical multidimensionality of life: Oprah Winfrey, Dexter Morgan, Bill O'Reilly, Alisha Florek, Detective Bobby Goren, Liz Lemon, Damien Lewis, Jon Stewart, Jack Bauer, Shawn Carter, Patrick Jane, Dr. Gregory House, and Ned Stark, who always kept it real.

Gratitude to the divine goddess that is the Chopra Center for Wellbeing.

ABOUT THE AUTHOR

As the Lead Educator of the Chopra Center for Wellbeing in Carlsbad, California, **davidji** apprenticed for nearly a decade under Drs. Deepak Chopra and David Simon and was appointed the first Dean of Chopra Center University. He is a Chopra Center Certified Vedic Master, Primordial Sound Meditation Instructor, Perfect Health Ayurvedic Lifestyle Teacher, a Seven Spiritual Laws of Yoga Instructor, a world-renowned creator of guided meditations, and the host of *LIVE from the Sweetspot with davidji* on Hay House Radio.

davidji is an internationally recognized life guide, author, meditation recording artist, motivational speaker, and meditation instructor. He travels the world sharing timeless wisdom on cultivating a spiritual practice, modern-day stress management, emotional healing techniques, work/life balance, and finding deeper self-fulfillment. His dharma, or life's purpose, is to help individuals awaken to the best version of themselves and discover their finest expression in life. *Secrets of Meditation* is a Nautilus Silver Award winner and among the 2013 Better Books for a Better World.

To join the davidji Meditation Community, visit **davidji.com**.

davidji

transform the world *by transforming yourself*

visit davidji.com

For more information on meditation, conscious choice-making, stress management, heart healing, and integrating timeless wisdom into your daily life, visit www.davidji.com.

join the davidji sweetspot community

Sign up at davidji.com to be a member of the davidji sweetspot community, and receive regular tools, tips, and techniques to lesson stress, ease anxiety, and bring greater balance into your life including free meditations, stress busters, and ways to connect with the millions of meditators around the world.

follow davidji

 facebook.com/flowoflove
twitter.com/intothegap

Hay House Titles of Related Interest

YOU CAN HEAL YOUR LIFE, the movie, starring Louise L. Hay & Friends
(available as a 1-DVD program and an expanded 2-DVD set)
Watch the trailer at: **www.LouiseHayMovie.com**

THE SHIFT, the movie,
starring Dr. Wayne W. Dyer
(available as a 1-DVD program and an expanded 2-DVD set)
Watch the trailer at: **www.DyerMovie.com**

AWAKENING THE LUMINOUS MIND: Tibetan Meditation for Inner Peace and Joy, by Tenzin Wangyal Rinpoche

EUFEELING! The Art of Creating Inner Peace and Outer Prosperity, by Dr. Frank J. Kinslow

GRACE, GUIDANCE, AND GIFTS: Sacred Blessings to Light Your Way, by Sonia Choquette

THE MINDFUL MANIFESTO: How Doing Less and Noticing More Can Help Us Thrive in a Stressed-Out World, by Dr. Jonty Heaversedge and Ed Halliwell

A MINDFUL NATION: How a Simple Practice Can Help Us Reduce Stress, Improve Performance, and Recapture the American Spirit, by Congressman Tim Ryan

SOUL-CENTERED: Transform Your Life in 8 Weeks with Meditation, by Sarah McLean

All of the above are available at your local bookstore,
or may be ordered by contacting Hay House (see next page).

We hope you enjoyed this Hay House book. If you'd like to receive our online catalog featuring additional information on Hay House books and products, or if you'd like to find out more about the Hay Foundation, please contact:

Hay House, Inc., P.O. Box 5100, Carlsbad, CA 92018-5100
(760) 431-7695 or (800) 654-5126
(760) 431-6948 (fax) or (800) 650-5115 (fax)
www.hayhouse.com® • **www.hayfoundation.org**

Published and distributed in Australia by: Hay House Australia Pty. Ltd., 18/36 Ralph St., Alexandria NSW 2015 • *Phone:* 612-9669-4299 *Fax:* 612-9669-4144 • www.hayhouse.com.au

Published and distributed in the United Kingdom by: Hay House UK, Ltd., Astley House • 33 Notting Hill Gate, London W11 3JQ *Phone:* 44-20-3675-2450 • *Fax:* 44-20-3675-2451 www.hayhouse.co.uk

Published and distributed in the Republic of South Africa by: Hay House SA (Pty), Ltd., P.O. Box 990, Witkoppen 2068 *Phone/Fax:* 27-11-467-8904 • www.hayhouse.co.za1

Published in India by: Hay House Publishers India, Muskaan Complex, Plot No. 3, B-2, Vasant Kunj, New Delhi 110 070 • *Phone:* 91-11-4176-1620 *Fax:* 91-11-4176-1630 • www.hayhouse.co.in

Distributed in Canada by: Raincoast, 9050 Shaughnessy St., Vancouver, B.C. V6P 6E5 • *Phone:* (604) 323-7100 • *Fax:* (604) 323-2600 • www.raincoast.com

Take Your Soul on a Vacation

Visit **www.HealYourLife.com®** to regroup, recharge, and reconnect with your own magnificence. Featuring blogs, mind-body-spirit news, and life-changing wisdom from Louise Hay and friends.

Visit **www.HealYourLife.com** today!